CALGARY'S MOUNTAIN PANORAMA

text by DAVE BIRREL
artwork by RON ELLIS

Acknowledgements

Bill Watt, Eileen Malmberg, Ian Halladay, Isamay
Ballachey and Wayne Arnold have all been very helpful
in supplying information included in this book.
Milt Magee and Tom Hornecker, who know well the
pleasure of looking at distant peaks, have also made
significant contributions. I also wish to acknowledge
Ken Jones and Don King whose memories of earlier
days in these mountains have been most inspiring.
A special thankyou to my father, Dr. John Birrell, who
told me about the Sawback Range.
The publisher wishes to acknowledge the support of
Alberta Culture and the Alberta Foundation for the
Literary Arts in the production of this book.

© Dave Birrell 1990

All rights reserved. No part of this work may be
reproduced or transmitted in any form or by any means,
electronic or mechanical, including photocopying and
recording, or by any information storage or retrieval
system, except as may be expressly permitted in writing
from the publisher.

Published by Rocky Mountain Books
106 Wimbledon Crescent, Calgary, Alberta

Printed and bound in Canada by
Imprimerie Gagné Ltée., Quebec

Canadian Cataloguing in Publication Data

Birrell, Dave, 1944-
Calgary's mountain panorama

ISBN 0-921102-12-7
1. Rocky Mountains, Canadian (B.C. and
Alta.) - Description and travel.* I. Ellis,
Ron, 1943-   II. Title.
FC219.B57 1990   917.123'3   C90-091143-3
F1090.B57 1990

CALGARY AND ITS MOUNTAINS

An enduring relationship

*"Never will I forget the sight that met our eyes - the confluence
of the two winding rivers with their wooded banks, the verdant
valley, and beyond, the wide expanse of green plain that
stretched itself in homage to the distant blue mountains."*

This memory was related to the Calgary Herald by G. C. King, a
member of the North West Mounted Police's F Troop which had
halted on high ground above the north bank of the Bow Valley in
the late summer of 1875. Their leading officer, Inspector Brisbois,
was convinced that here was the site for the fort required midway
between Macleod and Fort Edmonton. Much has changed in the
valley since that day, but the view of the *"distant blue mountains"*
remains just as F Troop saw it and is still just as impressive to
Calgarians and their visitors.

An 1885 publication entitled, "Calgary, Her Industries and
Resources" was prepared to encourage visitors to *"remain at
Calgary"*. Clearly designed to encourage business and industrial
growth, the document reflects early interest in the mountains by
referring to the city as a base for the exploitation of coal and the
"treasures" stored up in the mountains where the *"precious and
valuable metals are being worked up by enterprising capitalists."*

However, even in this publication it was pointed out that there
was more to the mountain presence than the potential for profit.
The view of the mountains from Calgary was described as
"majestic to sublimity."

Today, Calgary's mountains still play a role in attracting people
to the city and, in addition, provide a symbol of the city's history,
western spirit, and vitality.

But most importantly, Calgary's enduring mountain panorama is
a continuing source of quiet, personal pleasure for its citizens.

GEOLOGY AND THE MOUNTAIN VIEW
The rock layers below southern Alberta

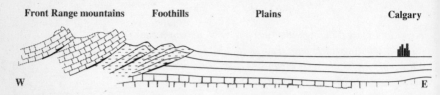

The surface of the plains of southern Alberta is generally covered with fairly recent deposits related to the melting of the last ice age approximately 12,000 years ago. Lake sediments and glacial stream deposits together with till cover much of Alberta to a depth of 10 to 20 metres. Till consists of unsorted material deposited directly from glacial ice and ranges in size from very fine clay to large boulders such as the Big Rock west of Okotoks.

To understand the geology of the mountains shown on the Panorama, one must know that the bedrock lying below the glacial deposits is from four geologic eras. The first layers of sedimentary rock are of the Cenozoic Era and were deposited in shallow seas 50 to 65 million years ago just after the dinosaurs became extinct and prior to the rise to prominence of the mammals. The sandstones and shales are about 500 m thick below the City of Calgary and extend west only to the edge of the foothills.

Below the rock layers of the Cenozoic Era lie those of the older Mesozoic Era. Primarily sandstones and shales, these rocks were deposited during the Age of the Dinosaurs from 225 million years ago until 65 million years ago and are about 2,000 m thick.

Limestone is the dominant rock type of the Paleozoic Era which lies beneath the Mesozoic layers. These rocks were deposited in seas from 570 million years ago until the Mesozioc Era began 225 million years ago during the time when life evolved from very simple forms to include fish, amphibians, and reptiles. The Paleozoic layer is approximately 1,000 m thick below the City of Calgary.

The oldest of the four geologic eras is the Precambrian. Life at this time consisted only of very simple forms such as algae, bacteria, worms and sponges. This layer is an extension of the Canadian Shield and consists of both metamorphic and igneous rocks.

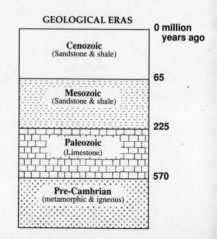

Mountain building

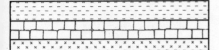

A - The layers of sedimentary rock were deposited in shallow seas on top of the Pre-cambrian. Paleozoic layers were deposited first, followed by the Mesozoic layers.

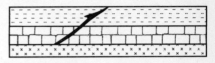

B - About 80 million years ago great pressures from the west began to break the Mesozoic and Cenozoic rock layers and fault lines were formed.

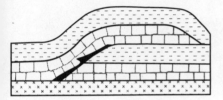

C - The pressure continued and forced the older Paleozoic rock to slide along the low angled fault lines up and over layers of younger rock. The amount of movement was several tens of kilometres.

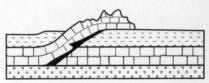

D - About 40 million years ago the pressure subsided and the mountain building was complete. Since that time, erosion by glacial activity and water has removed great volumes of rock to leave the landscape we see today.

Erosion

The younger Mesozoic rock layers are composed primarily of sandstone and shale, comparatively soft and easily eroded rock types. Since they tend to wear away relatively quickly, they leave rounded, smoothly-graded slopes like the dark, gently contoured, tree-covered foothills one can see below the peaks of the Panorama.

Although Mesozoic rocks do form some minor summits in the front ranges, it is the Paleozoic limestones that form the high peaks. This is because limestone is a much harder rock than shale and sandstone and consequently erodes more slowly and tends to form cliffs. All the towering grey cliffs which form the skyline of Calgary's Rocky Mountain Panorama are formed by the hard limestones of this era. These mountains, then, are of the same layer which lies from 2,500 to 3,000 m beneath the City of Calgary.

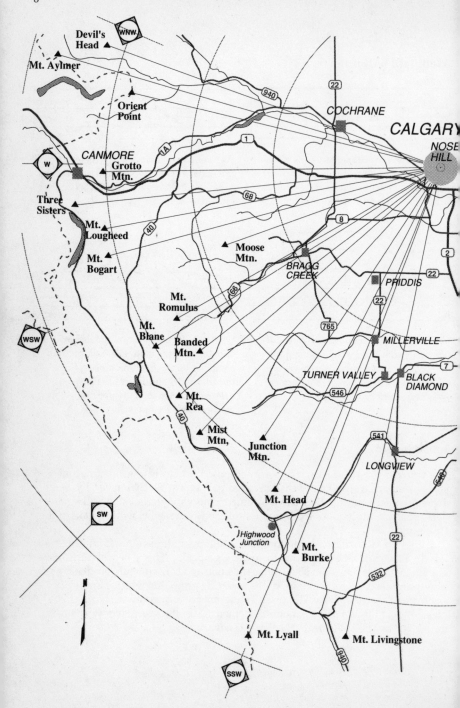

THE PANORAMA DRAWING
and how to use it

The Panorama was drawn from the top of Nose Hill in north Calgary at a point north of the junction of 19th Street West and John Laurie Boulevard. This is the finest natural location in the city for viewing the mountains. From other locations, many mountains, particularly those in the front ranges, can still be easily identified but the more distant peaks may be shifted considerably in relation to the closer ones. In addition, some of the distant mountains visible from the hilltop may be hidden behind closer mountains when viewed from a lower elevation.

It should be noted that some points on the Panorama which appear very striking are not the tops of significant mountains at all. The angle of viewing is critical as the orientation and appearance of various high ridges and subsidiary summits changes quickly.

Some of the 54 peaks on the Panorama are difficult to identify particularly during less than ideal viewing conditions. However, there are 11 mountains which for a variety of reasons are easily identifiable from Nose Hill and from other locations as well. From south to north they are Mount Head, Mist Mountain, Mount Rae, Banded Peak, Mount Cornwall, Mount Glasgow, Mount Romulus, Moose Mountain, Mount Bogart, Mount Lougheed, and Devil's Head. Once one becomes familiar with these 11, other less distinctive peaks may be identified in relation to them.

By using the Panorama and studying the mountains at different times of the year and during various weather conditions within the mountains, one's understanding of what can be seen from Calgary will be greatly increased. In summer, clear, crisp mornings are best for viewing distant peaks before afternoon haziness limits visibility. The most interesting conditions occur when patchy cloudiness produces a quickly changing scene with some peaks in shadow and others spotlighted by sunshine. When distant peaks and ranges are completely obscured by storms and clouds, the outlines of closer mountains such as Moose and Blackrock become very prominent. Snow cover, particularly in the late spring and early fall, will usually highlight the higher and more distant peaks. Mount Lyall, the Misty Range, Mount Bogart, and Mount Aylmer are often snowcapped when the lower and nearer mountains are bare. Occasionally though, a portion of the front range will receive a snowfall that the others will not. Banded Peak, Mount Cornwall, and Mount Glasgow seem particularly susceptible to this phenomenon.

Hopefully, this book will enable you to identify some of your favorite peaks on the Panorama, learn a little bit about them, and then be able to locate them again while driving on our mountain highways.

Mountain Checklist

- ❏ Coffin Mountain
- ❏ Mount Livingstone
- ❏ Hailstone Butte
- ❏ Plateau Mountain
- ❏ Mount Burke
- ❏ Mount Lyall
- ❏ Mount Gass
- ❏ Holy Cross Mountain
- ❏ Mount Head
- ❏ Mount Pyriform
- ❏ Junction Mountain
- ❏ Gibraltar Mountain
- ❏ Mist Mountain
- ❏ Bluerock Mountain
- ❏ Storm Mountain
- ❏ Mount Burns
- ❏ Mount Rae
- ❏ Cougar Mountain
- ❏ Forget-Me-Not Mountain
- ❏ Mount Foch
- ❏ Banded Peak
- ❏ Elpoca Mountain
- ❏ Tombstone Mountain
- ❏ Mount Cornwall
- ❏ Mount Glasgow
- ❏ Mount Blane
- ❏ Mount Brock
- ❏ Mount Hood
- ❏ Mount Remus
- ❏ Mount Romulus
- ❏ Mount Evan-Thomas
- ❏ Fisher Peak
- ❏ Prairie Mountain
- ❏ Nihahi Ridge
- ❏ Mount Howard
- ❏ Moose Mountain
- ❏ Mount McDougall
- ❏ Mount Kidd
- ❏ Mount Bogart
- ❏ Mount Sparrowhawk
- ❏ Wind Mountain
- ❏ Mount Allan
- ❏ Mount Lougheed
- ❏ Mount Lorette
- ❏ The Three Sisters
- ❏ Grotto Mountain
- ❏ Mount John Laurie
- ❏ Association Peak
- ❏ End Mountain
- ❏ Saddle Peak
- ❏ Orient Point
- ❏ Mount Aylmer
- ❏ Devil's Head
- ❏ Blackrock Mountain

THE PANORAMA FROM NOSE HILL

The pleasure of understanding the view

After assisting in the early mapping of the Rockies, a surveyor eloquently described his enjoyment of a mountain view when he wrote, "*I know well the thrill of viewing the august panorama of peaks circling the horizon, to see here and there peaks one has known before and occasionally, in the dim distance, big fellows one has climbed years ago. It is like re-encountering old friends and by this widening circle of alpine landmarks one's knowledge of the country is enhanced and takes form.*"

A knowledge of Calgary's Mountain Panorama provides one with the opportunity to relate the view to the geography within the mountains; the pleasure of knowing where the rivers flow and what lies on the other side of a peak. In addition, a sense of history is gained through a knowledge of who named these mountains and why, and of some of the events which have taken place on their slopes or nearby.

A surprising number and variety of people can be related in a very direct way to the peaks of Calgary's Panorama. Explorers, businessmen, a Governor General, authors, ranchers, forest rangers, botanists, geologists, generals, admirals, surveyors, missionaries, a soldier, climbers, politicians, a lawyer, and professors are all a part of the history of these mountains we see from Calgary.

In addition, we can see mountains named after warships, animals, a flower, characters from Roman Mythology, the site of a World War I battle, and a small town in Quebec.

The following pages introduce the 54 mountains which comprise the view from Nose Hill. They are discussed in the order in which they appear on the Panorama, from left to right beginning with Coffin Mountain.

Although Coffin Mountain appears to be the southernmost peak, Mount Lyall, which is 8 km farther away on the Continental Divide, is actually 2 km farther south, directly west of a point 7 km north of Claresholm. The northernmost point on the Panorama is an unnamed peak at the northern end of a small range which lies somewhat to the east of the main trend of the front ranges and is directly west of the town of Crossfield. The headwaters of Burnt Timber Creek lie to the north and west of this small range. The distance from Mount Lyall to the northern end of the Panorama is 158 kilometres.

The closest mountain which we can see from Nose Hill is Moose Mountain, only 55 km to the west-southwest. Mount Lyall is the most distant at 121 kilometres.

Twelve of the mountains identified have elevations in excess of 3,000 m, the highest being Mount Rae at 3,225 m. The lowest mountain on the Panorama is Prairie Mountain at 2,205 metres.

Accompanying the information on the individual peaks seen from Nose Hill are drawings which show each mountain as it may be seen from an easily accessible viewpoint on a paved, numbered highway. Thus the peaks which may be identified from Calgary with the assistance of the Panorama may also be viewed from much closer quarters and from a different perspective.

COFFIN MOUNTAIN
2,407 m 113 km

Lying only 10 degrees west of south, Coffin Mountain is the southernmost peak in the front range visible from Nose Hill. The Livingstone Range, of which it is a part, has no significant mountains south of Coffin Mountain until Thunder Mountain rises to 2,352 m beyond the Oldman River 31 km to the south. From Beaver Pass to the north of the mountain, Beaver Creek flows west into the Livingstone River.

When its entire length is viewed from the east, the mountain's profile resembles a casket with the head to the north and the feet to the south.

View to the west from the Bar Eleven Gate on Highway #22, 4.6 km south of the junction with Highway #533

The gate at the entrance to the Bar Eleven Ranch south of Chain Lakes on Highway #22 is a good viewpoint for both Coffin Mountain (left) and Mount Livingstone (centre). As well, Sheep Mountain (far left) may be seen in front of Coffin Mountain, and Saddle Mountain (far right) in front and to the right of Mount Livingstone. Between Coffin and Livingstone lies Beaver Pass, through which a high ridge west of Highway #940 can be seen in the distance.

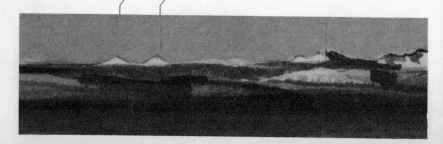

MOUNT LIVINGSTONE
2,422 m 110 km

The Livingstone Range extends for a distance of almost 100 km from the Highwood River to the Crowsnest River and is the easternmost range of the Rockies. Since the mountains are approximately 400 m lower than those seen more directly west and southwest of Calgary and are located 95 km or more from Nose Hill, they appear quite small on the Panorama. Notice how Mount Livingstone and Coffin Mountain are similar in profile and form twin peaks. The reason for this particular mountain being named Mount Livingstone is not known, for it is neither the highest nor the most impressive peak of the Livingstone Range.

Dr. David Livingstone in 1852

The range was named in 1858 by Captain Blakiston of the Palliser Expedition for the British explorer, geographer, and missionary who remade a large part of the map of the Dark Continent. Dr. David Livingstone was understandably revered by John Palliser who felt privileged to have sat beside him at a meeting of the Royal Geographical Society. For 32 years Livingstone travelled up and down Africa from the Cape to the equator and from the Atlantic to the Indian Ocean laying the foundation for British title in many areas.

During the course of his travels Dr. Livingstone survived an attack by a lion, *"Growling horribly close to my ear,"* wrote Livingstone, *"he shook me as a terrier dog does a rat. The shock produced a stupor similar to that which seems to be felt by a mouse after the first shake of a cat. It caused a sort of dreaminess, in which there was no sense of pain nor feeling of terror, though I was quite conscious of all that was happening."*

Fortunately for Livingstone, the lion left him to attack another member of the party.

Livingstone wanted desperately to find the source of the Nile River and was still trying when he died in 1873 following a severe attack of dysentery with complications brought on by excessive hardships.

HAILSTONE BUTTE
2,363 m 103 km

Although Hailstone Butte appears farther south than Plateau Mountain on the Panorama, it is actually 4 km directly east. Sentinel Pass, which lies between the two at the headwaters of Pekisko Creek, was formerly used as a route for moving cattle into forestry grazing leases in the mountains to the west, but nowadays is not nearly as heavily travelled as another Sentinel Pass which is one of the highest and most spectacular hikes in the Lake Louise area. Sentinel Peak, although not identified on the Panorama, may be seen with the aid of binoculars just at the left edge of Plateau.

This broad, smoothly-contoured mountain is often difficult to distinguish from Plateau Mountain when viewed from the prairies. It lies to the north of Highway #532 which climbs from the east to an elevation of 2,027 m at a pass, known locally as The Hump, below the mountain's southern slopes.

The summit is the site of an Alberta Forest Service lookout. The lookout system was established in the 1920's and despite the advent of a satellite assisted lightning monitoring system will probably be in use for some years to come.

When Hailstone Butte Lookout was built in 1952, roads were bulldozed to lookout sites and an ugly Z-shaped scar was left on the eastern slope below the summit of the mountain. As well as damaging vegetation, the road also provided access to delicate alpine areas for misguided hunters who took delight in shooting the marmots near the summit.

The original wooden lookout on Hailstone was replaced by a prefab metal structure in 1979.

View to the west from Wilson's Gate on Highway #22, 0.9 km south of the junction with Highway #533

PLATEAU MOUNTAIN
2,514 m 102 km

Even from a distance of over 100 km the reason for this mountain's name is obvious. Known locally as Flat-top, it can hardly be referred to as a peak since its summit is more or less flat for a distance of 8 km from north to south. It is separated from Mount Burke by Salter Pass and lies immediately to the east of Highway #940 south of Cataract Creek.

An interesting feature of Plateau Mountain is the extensive areas of patterned ground where larger pieces of rock have accumulated into polygonal patterns surrounding finer materials in the centre. This phenomenon is thought to have been caused by a cracking of the ground due to cooling which produces a series of surface fissures such as those seen on a dried-out mud puddle.

The reason for the sorting of the surface rocks to correspond with the cracks is less clearly understood. At any rate, the patterned ground on Plateau Mountain was probably formed during the ice age when the mountain, like most of the peaks on the Panorama, stood above the surrounding ice surface as a nunatak.

Patterned ground on Plateau Mountain
(Photo Gillean Daffern)

Plateau is the only mountain on the Panorama whose summit is visited on a regular basis all year long.

HAILSTONE BUTTE   **PLATEAU MTN.**

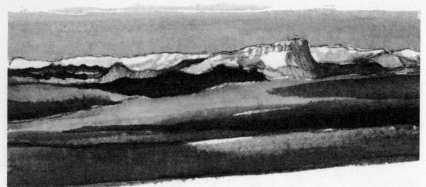

View to the southwest from Highway #22, 20 km south of Longview

The mountain is easily identified from the prairies to the east but one can get a closer view from Highway #22 although parts of the mountain are hidden behind Sentinel Peak and Hailstone Butte.

Drilling rig on Plateau Mountain, 1957 (photo by Mrs. A. Hogg; courtesy Tales and Trails History Book Society)

Of the eight producing gas wells in the Savannah Creek Field, two are located right on top of the mountain and require the access road kept plowed throughout the winter months for Husky Oil personnel.

Because soft limestone has numerous caverns, seepages, and underground streams, severe lost circulation problems plagued the drilling of the first well in the 1950's. Dumping tree boughs, cement and truckloads of asphalt and sawdust down the hole failed to stop the drilling fluid from escaping.

MOUNT BURKE
2,545 m 95 km

Two broad shoulders with a symmetric summit in between characterize this peak which is the second tallest in the Livingstone Range and only 6 m lower than Centre Peak which lies 13 km northeast of Coleman at the other end of the range. Located south of the Highwood Valley, Mount Burke lies directly east of Cataract Creek's headwaters which flow towards the mountain before turning north to a confluence with the Highwood River.

The summit was the site of one of the first fire lookouts built by the Alberta Forest Service in 1929. To protect the building and its inhabitant from lightning, steel cables ran from a post on the roof to a main cable which extended 1.5 km down the mountain to be grounded in moist earth. Thus the building was said to be safe if the telephone line which connected the lookout with the Forestry Station building below was disconnected. One Lookout forgot to disconnect the phone. Entering through the phone line, a charge of lightning exploded the bed, leaving it in small pieces, and broke a hole in a window as the forgetful resident sat beside it. It is said that the Lookout, who had admitted to being afraid of lightning berfore he went up, burst out the door and descended Mount Burke as quickly as possible never to return. Known as Cameron Lookout, it operated until 1953 when it was replaced by lower, more easily serviced lookouts on Raspberry Ridge and Hailstone Butte.

Burke Mountain Lookout c. 1930's (courtesy Nanton and District Historical Society)

D. C. Burke was a NWMP veteran who established a small ranch on Pekisko Creek at the foot of the mountain. Official records show that Mount Burke was named in his honour by a survey crew mapping the area in the early 1900's. However, Mr. Burk's granddaughter recalls being told that the mountain was, in fact, named after Mrs. Burke whose excellant meals and hospitality were enjoyed by the survey crew.

Mount Burke is easily recognizable from the Highwood Trail (#541) near the Stampede Ranch, but is most impressive when viewed from the east on Highway #22 where, with binoculars, one can still see the old lookout building clinging to the very top of the mountain.

MOUNT LYALL
2,952 m 121 km

It is not possible to get close to Mount Lyall on a paved highway, but the view to the west-southwest from the overpass on Highway #2, 19 km south of High River is striking, the peak (centre) appearing as a broad, symmetric triangle often snow-covered

Mount Lyall is the most distant peak visible from Nose Hill and the most southerly even though several other mountains to its left on the Panorama appear to be farther south. Both Lyall and Mount Gass just to the north are part of the High Rock Range which forms the Continental Divide from Weary Creek Gap (west of Holy Cross Mountain) to the Crowsnest Pass. From headwaters between the two mountains, the Oldman River flows south past the eastern slopes of the mountain. Despite its distance from Calgary and the mountain's location on the divide, one can see almost the full height of Mount Lyall because the line of sight is through Highwood Gap and then up the broad valley between the Livingstone and High Rock Ranges.

Dr. David Lyall was a surgeon with the British Boundary Commission which mapped the border with the United States from the Prairies to the Pacific between 1858 and 1862. Since the mountain lies some distance from the border, it was likely named to honour his work as a naturalist with a particular interest in alpine plants rather than his contribution to mapping.

During his time in Canada Lyall sent some 1,375 species of plants back to the Royal Botanical Gardens at Kew, England. Some he chose to name after himself, the most well known of which is the Alpine or Lyall's Larch which almost defines the alpine zone in the southern Alberta Rockies south of the Bow Valley. This tree grows between 1,900 and 2,100 m and has light green, soft needles which turn a beautiful golden colour in fall and are shed. Another plant Dr. Lyall chose to name after himself is Lyall's Saxifrage. Often growing in dense masses in wet moss beside alpine brooks, the small delicate flowers are white with yellow spots.

Lyall's Saxifrage

MOUNT GASS
(2,866 m   118 km)

Mount Gass is located to the north of Gass Pass and together with Mount Lyall to the south is one of the two most distant peaks on the Panorama. Although similar in profile, Gass is more smoothly-contoured and symmetric with a rounded summit.

King Bearspaw was a Stoney Indian who became familiar with the mountains at the head of the Oldman River. During his explorations in the early part of the century he noticed some unusual rocks high on the eastern slopes of Mount Gass and decades later mentioned them to Bill Watt and some friends from Nanton who had some knowledge of prospecting. In 1948 they staked a claim on the mountainside, realizing that the interesting rocks contained galena, a lead ore, as well as silver, zinc, and even traces of gold. Western Canadian Colleries were also in the Upper Oldman Valley exploring for coal but took notice of Bill's samples, followed the tracks to the site, and eventually gained control of the lease and established a mine. Handpicked pieces of rock were extracted from the mine tunneled some 15 m into the mountain side, loaded into boxes, and winched up a chute over the east ridge of the mountain to a very rough road. The operation was very small scale and continued for a few years in the 1950's until it was determined to be uneconomic.

Many of the mountains of the Elk and High Rock Ranges honour Canadian servicemen who died during the First World War. Some, such as Mount Bishop in the Upper Highwood, were named after well known heroes such as Billy Bishop who won the Victoria Cross shooting down 72 enemy aircraft, while others seem to be named after more ordinary soldiers.

L. H. Gass was a survey assistant killed in action in 1917. As the survey to define the BC-Alberta boundary was taking place during and after the war, it probably presented an opportunity on someone's part to commemorate a friend and associate.

King Bearspaw (left) with Sam Rider (Glenbow Archives)

Mount Gass, as is the case with three other peaks on the Panorama, cannot be seen from a nearby highway.

MT. LYALL

HOLY CROSS MOUNTAIN
2,667 m 85 km

Holy Cross Mountain is the southernmost peak most easily identifiable from many areas of Calgary with an elevation less than that of Nose Hill. It is also the southernmost mountain of the Highwood Range which extends north to Gibraltar Mountain in the Sheep River Valley.

*View to the west from Stampede Ranch,
21.6 km west of Longview on Highway #541*

Between the Highwood Range to the east and the High Rock Range to the west, the Highwood River flows southwest for 23 km before swinging sharply to the east and passing through narrow Highwood Gap below the southern slopes of Holy Cross. Below the gap the river continues east through beautiful foothills ranching country to Longview and High River, eventually flowing into the Bow.

When the mountain is viewed from the southeast as spring snows are melting, a large cross of snow often appears on the upper slopes. This feature can be quite striking, but some years it never appears and at best only lasts for a week or two. The Cross was undoubtedly noticed by Raymond Patterson, a rancher and author who lived in the foothills below Holy Cross.

The Rockies were the worst named range in the world according to Raymond Patterson. As evidence of this he wrote, *"If you look carefully at the map you can find there, enthroned in stone, a collaborator, a traitor to his country, sundry generals of dubious merit, and a demagogue who, for his own ends, wrecked a way of life which had taken centuries to perfect - to cite only a few of these ill-named mountains."*

In his book "The Buffalo Head" Patterson refused to accept the official name of Mount McPhail; instead he referred to this peak in the Upper Highwood as "The Pyramid" which it closely resembles. He must have taken some solace in that Holy Cross, the mountain nearest his beloved Buffalo Head Ranch, had such a suitable and natural name. Perhaps it was Patterson himself who suggested its name, although the name was not officially approved by the provincial authorities until 1980.

Raymond Patterson in 1966 (Photo by Palmer Lewis; courtesy Marigold Patterson)

Patterson, owner of the Buffalo Head Ranch during the 1930's, wrote two best-selling books recounting his extensive travels in the Highwood-Kananaskis area when it was still pristine wilderness. He was deeply affected by the great Phillip's Fire of 1936 which burned through the Highwood Valley. The fire, combined with the building of a major road which Patterson described as a *"dusty, ill-omened snake"* signalled the end of an era, and during an October in the mid 1940's, Patterson and his wife sold the ranch and with three packhorses rode over the Highwood and North Kananaskis Passes to continue their lives in British Columbia.

HOLY CROSS MTN.

MOUNT HEAD
2,781 m 83 km

Mount Head lies only 3 km north of Holy Cross Mountain, the two standing side by side on the Panorama and having similar profiles when viewed from Calgary.

Mount Head has two distinct summits when viewed from the southwest near the entrance to Eden Valley Indian Reservation on Highwood Trail (#541). The western summit is the higher of the two; the eastern summit has the "head."

Raymond Patterson made the first ascent in 1934.

Mount Head's most distinctive feature is the striking profile of a head in the northern cliffs of the eastern summit. Although this cannot be seen from Nose Hill, once recognised it is quite noticeable from the prairies to the east and southeast of the mountain.

The mountain was named by John Palliser who must have regarded it as a prominent landmark as it appears on his 1860 map. However, he placed it in error on the sharp angle of the Continental Divide south of Kananaskis Lakes at the location of what is now known as Mount Tyrwhitt. Although surveyors of the late 1800's made the correction, his error continued to be published in some atlases as late as the 1920's.

John Palliser led the British North American Exploring Expedition which from 1857 to 1860 was charged with the task of exploring, studying, and mapping the plains between the North Saskatchewan River and the American border, as well as the southern passes through the Rockies. Also included in the party were Thomas Blakiston (magnetic observer), Dr. James Hector (geologist and naturalist), Eugene Bourgeau (botanist), and John Sullivan (astronomical observer). The expedition amassed much scientific data describing the country, its fauna and flora, inhabitants, and possibilities for settlement and for some time the maps and reports were the major source of information regarding southern Canada from Lake Superior to the Okanagan Valley of British Columbia.

View to the northwest from 0.6 km west of the bridge to the Eden Valley Indian Reserve, 24.9 km west of Longview on Highway #541

John Palliser's father was an old friend of Sir Edmund Head who at the time he was Governor General of British North America encouraged Palliser and even gave him a retrieving dog to take on the expedition. Although records indicate that Mount Head was named by Palliser in honour of Sir Edmund, the "head" just below the eastern summit is another very obvious explanation for the name as it continues to gaze towards the northern skies. Either way, the name was a most appropriate choice.

Capt. John Palliser (left) with Sir James Hector (Glenbow Archives)

MT. HEAD

MOUNT PYRIFORM
2,732 m 78 km

The Highwood Range stretches for some 27 km to the east of Highway #40 from Holy Cross Mountain in the south to Gibraltar Mountain in the north. Mount Pyriform and Junction Mountain are the only named peaks in a small group which lies several kilometres to the east of the middle portion of the main axis. The north-south flowing Junction Creek separates Mounts Pyriform and Junction from the rest of the Highwood Range.

Mount Pyriform, which is the southernmost and the higher of the two, was named after its pyramid-shaped peak.

View to the northwest from Stampede Ranch, 21.6 km west of Longview on Highway #541

Another mountain located just 1.5 km to the south rises to within 30 m of Mount Pyriform's summit. Although very prominent in the view from the east and southeast, it remains unnamed.

JUNCTION MOUNTAIN
2,650 m 74 km

The smooth upper slopes of Junction Mountain form a distinctive tri-angular-shaped snowfield during the winter. This, together with a long, gently-sloped ridge leading off to the south of the mountain are the best ways to recognize this peak from the prairies.

Bluerock and Junction Creeks join the Sheep River within a few hundred metres of each other and it is probable that these confluences are the reason for the naming of Junction Creek. Since the mountain is located 7 km to the south of this junction, it was likely named after the creek rather than vice versa.

For a closer view, drive west on Sheep River Trail (#546) to its end at Junction Creek Day-Use Area. From this point, Junction Mountain may be seen by looking south up Junction Creek Valley. The mountain forms the valley's eastern slope, the western slopes being formed by the main portion of the Highwood Range.

Junction Fire Lookout (Photo Gillean Daffern)

North of the headwaters of Coal Creek, a high grassy ridge extends 4 km to the west where it abuts against the eastern cliffs of Junction Mountain. Located on the east end of the ridge is the Junction Fire Lookout. Three buildings have occupied the site, the most recently constructed being a prefab metal structure.

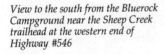
View to the south from the Bluerock Campground near the Sheep Creek trailhead at the western end of Highway #546

GIBRALTAR MOUNTAIN
2,665 m 77 km

The British have used the famous "Rock of Gibraltar" to guard the western entrance to the Mediterranean Sea since the early 1700's. When viewed from Calgary, and from most other points, this peak has no resemblance at all to the famous Rock. However, when travelling up the Sheep River west of Turner Valley, the reason for its name is very obvious. Although the near vertical and in places overhanging cliffs of the north face are the most impressive aspect of the mountain, the actual summit is another 1.5 km to the west.

The mountain lies directly west of High River. When driving west from the town towards Hartell on Highway #543, one is heading directly towards the cliffs which can be very conspicuous when background mountains are white because of snow or clouds.

The original Rock of Gibraltar

While there are easy ways to get to the summit of Gibraltar Mountain, the north face is a real mountaineering challenge. It was first climbed in 1971 by Bill Davidson and Jim White who took eight and one-half days to complete what was the first "extended aid" climb in the Canadian Rockies.

In the summer of 1918 the mountain was the scene of a tragic accident. Three young men who were working at the Burns coal mine in the Sheep Valley climbed to the top of the mountain which at that time was known locally as "Sheer Cliff." One of them, a visitor from the west coast named Patterson, was approaching the cliff edge when a gust of wind forced him over the precipice. The body was never found. Over four decades later a trunk containing his personal belongings was discovered in a corner of one of the old mining town's buildings when it was about to be burned down.

The farther one drives towards the west on Sheep River Trail (#546) west of Turner Valley the more impressive the view of Gibraltar Mountain becomes, but it is not until Bluerock Recreation Area is reached that one is treated to an unobstructed look at the full cliff face

View to the west from the Bluerock Recreation Area near the western end of Highway #546

As the Sheep River flows southeast from its headwaters between Mount Rae and Cougar Mountain, it heads directly towards the north end of the Highwood Range. As it reaches Gibraltar Mountain it turns to the east to flow out into the foothills. At this point, the 700 m vertical cliffs of the north face seem to create a mini-climate as north-facing slopes below receive very little direct sunlight and are completely covered with a healthy accumulation of moss unusual in the front ranges.

GIBRALTAR MTN.

MIST MOUNTAIN
3,138 m 84 km

Obviously high and distant, Mist Mountain is one of the most impressive and beautiful peaks in Calgary's Mountain Panorama and is most attractive when viewed from this direction. The rocky, vertical ribs which accentuate the steep east-facing cliffs are often highlighted by snow until mid-summer, and even without snow cover cast interesting shadows across the face.

Mist Mountain is the southernmost peak of the Misty Range which lies to the east of Highwood Pass on Kananaskis Trail (#40) and is the highest group of mountains whose individual summits (Mist Mountain, Storm Mountain, and Mount Rae) may be easily recognized from Calgary.

View to the northwest from Lantern Creek Picnic Site, 17.4 km north of Highwood Junction on Kananaskis Trail (#40)

The mountain dominates the view as one drives north on Kananaskis Trail (#40) from Highwood House. From this direction the fact that the Misty Range is a separate range is obvious when one sees Mist Mountain rising abruptly from the Highwood Valley. Mist Creek flows to the east of the mountain and Storm Creek flows to the west, the two creeks joining immediately south of the mountain to become the Highwood River.

East-facing cliffs of Mist Mountain, (Photo Gillean Daffern)

Located some 8 km west of the front range peaks of Mount Burns and Cougar Mountain, the peaks are often in cloud while the mountains closer to Calgary remain visible. They were supposedly hidden in mist when surveyor G. M. Dawson named the range and the mountain in 1884. There are some who believe that the name of the creek, range, and mountain are derived from the translation of the Indian word for mist. Possibly this Indian name referred to mists which form at times above a hot spring located in a remote part of the Mist Creek Valley.

The entire Misty range is made up of Mississippian Age rocks which are between 325 and 345 million years old. These rocks are very fossiliferous, containing numerous species the most outstanding of which is the solitary horn coral (right) which is cone-shaped and can grow to a length of 10 cm with a diameter of up to 5 cm.

MIST MTN.

During the 1940's before a road was built to Highwood Pass, Donald King and a group of friends from High River explored and climbed in the Highwood Valley. They began a tradition which lasted for several summers of camping on the summit of a mountain west of their home town and at a pre-arranged time and date shooting flares into the night sky. Hundreds of people in the area would assemble on hilltops and other suitable sites to watch the show which occurred precisely on the second as planned. At 11:00 pm on July 7th 1946, the launch site was the summit of Mist Mountain - the first recorded ascent of the mountain.

ON MISTY MOUNTAIN

I climbed to the top of a mountain,
Mounted God's stair to the skies;
I looked to the east with amazement,
Westward I stared in surprise;
I stood on the spire of a nation,
Held half a world in my eyes.

When sudden a cloud settled over,
Quickly the vapors rolled in
So silent, and eerily soundless,
Setting direction a-spin;
The sun was a full moon of crimson
Bright where the curtain held thin.

Somewhere to the east sprawled the prairie
Westward a peak-studded wall;
As shroudlike the white mists enveloped
My world in their foggy, wet pall;
I stood in the middle of nowhere,
Gazing at nothing at all.

Donald King (left) has written a book of poems "Beyond the Hills" relating to the Highwood Valley. The poem above was inspired by Mist Mountain
(1949 Photo courtesy of Donald King)

BLUEROCK MOUNTAIN
2,789 m 71 km

Threepoint Mountain, Mount Rose, and Bluerock Mountain form a small range lying to the east of the main front range peaks of Cougar Mountain and Mount Burns. All five of these mountains lie between the Elbow River and the Sheep River.

Bluerock Mountain is significantly higher than both Threepoint and Mount Rose and is the only one of the group which appears on the Panorama. It presents a smoothly-contoured profile and appears quite massive partly because it is 13 km closer to Calgary than is Mist Mountain which appears to its left.

The name is probably based on the fact that mountains like Bluerock, which are closer to a viewer on the prairies, appear darker or bluer than more distant peaks under hazy conditions.

View to the west from just beyond the Kananaskis Country Information Building on Highway #546, 18.5 km west of the junction with Highway #22

Bluerock Mountain is best seen from the Sheep River Valley where it appears somewhat in front and to the right of Mount Burns.

STORM MOUNTAIN
3,095 m 83 km

Storm Mountain is the middle of three major peaks making up the Misty Range. Although it appears on the Panorama just to the left of Mount Burns, it lies west of the Sheep River Valley some 8 km beyond Burns. It was named in 1884 by geologist George Dawson after a heavy rainfall occurred while he was camped to the west of the mountain.

Confusion sometimes occurs due to the presence of two Storm Mountains in the Rockies west of Calgary. The other one lies on the Continental Divide to the south of Vermillion Pass in Banff National Park.

Storm Creek flows from the western slopes of the mountain. Mist Creek flows east and then south below steep eastern cliffs to a beautiful meadow known as Misty Basin which contains one of the few remaining stands of mature spruce in the Kananaskis-Highwood area. The great fire of 1919 and the latest fire to rage in the area, the Phillip's Fire of 1936, somehow spared the upper reaches of the valley. The Phillip's Fire started in the Upper Elk Valley of British Columbia across the Continental Divide and for some reason was named after "Old Man Phillips" who had a cabin and guided hunting parties in the Upper Elk Valley for many years. With the hope of stopping the fire from coming across into Alberta, Freddy Nash the Sheep Creek forest ranger, asked permission to take men and supplies to McPhail Pass. The request was turned down by the Calgary Office and Nash was reprimanded for spending money on phone calls. Subsequently, the fire came through the pass and burned the Highwood Valley including much of the Mist Creek Valley below Storm and Mist Mountains until two or three days of rain extinguished the flames.

Almost all of the forests below the peaks of the Panorama are made up of Lodgepole Pine. The cones of this species of conifer release their seeds in vast numbers only when exposed to the very high temperature of a forest fire. Consequently, the newly seeded trees grow very close together and since they do not grow well in the shade the branches are crowded near the tree-tops. It is not a long-living tree and will gradually be replaced by spruce which, because it can grow in shade, will grow up through the pine and become the dominant tree – if fire does not interfere with the process. But it will be some time before this new generation of spruce reaches the age and magnificence of those in Misty Basin.

The best viewpoint for Storm Mountain is from Highwood Pass on Kananaskis Trail (#40). The contorted rock and vertical dips near the summit are highlighted by snow until late in the summer.

View to the southeast from Highwood Meadows parking lot on Highway #40, 17.7 km south of the junction with Kananaskis Lakes Trail

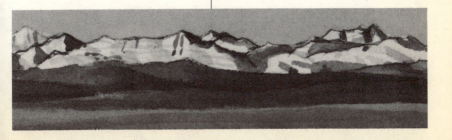

STORM MTN.

MOUNT BURNS
2,942 m 75 km

Patrick Burns in 1927 (Glenbow Archives)

Pat Burns is probably best known to Calgarians as one of the "Big Four" who organized the first Calgary Stampede in 1912. Together with A. E. Cross, A. J. McLean and George Lane, $100,000 worth of financing was arranged and the event billed as "The Greatest Outdoor Show on Earth."

Burns was also very successful as a pioneer of both the ranching and meat packing industries. However, the valley below the mountain that bears his name was the scene of one of his less successful business ventures. Around the turn of the century, Julius Rickert discovered coal in the Sheep River Valley to the south of what was to become Mount Burns. Rickert was able to interest Pat Burns in the project and with the influx of one million dollars in capital "P. Burns Coal Mines Limited" began operation in 1913. Although some coal was trucked out of the valley, most was stockpiled waiting for the arrival of the "Calgary and Southern Railway" which never came. During the clearing of the right-of-way for the planned railway, the great fire of 1919 was started and fanned by west winds, burned great tracts of land in the mountains and foothills.

Pat Burns made many trips through the foothills to his mine when the means of travel was by horseback. His employees wondered, at times why he went so often. In his book, "Pat Burns, Cattle King", Grant McEwan suggests that, *"there was a subtle reason, simply his love for the foothills, and in making a pack trip to Upper Sheep Creek he was finding the best possible release from business pressures and catching the summer and autumn glories of the back country."*

During the 1920's the demand for coal declined and the project shut down, leaving Pat Burns to concentrate on his other interests. The small town that had developed below Mount Burns was abandoned and the mine entrance sealed. The property continues to be held by the Burns Family, an island of private ownership in what is now Kananaskis Country. Some of the stockpiled coal remains to this day.

The entrance to Burns Mine, 1918 (Glenbow Archives)

View of Mt. Burns (left of centre) looking west from Highway #546, 10.4 km west of the Kananaskis Country Information Building

The Sheep River passes between Gibraltar Mountain to the south and Mount Burns to the north as it emerges into the foothills on its way to Okotoks and eventual confluence with the Highwood River. Immediately across the valley from the mountain, Burns Creek flows from the Misty Range, and above the old mine site discovered by Julius Rickert, Rickert's Pass connects the Sheep Valley with Mist Creek.

Mount Burns is not a particularly high mountain but it sprawls over a large area. When approaching along Sheep River Trail (#546) west of Turner Valley, one finds a good viewpoint just west of the Sheep River Ranger Station. The southern slopes of its more smoothly-contoured neighbour Bluerock Mountain are visible to the right of Mount Burns which is a complex peak and has several minor summits, some of which may be seen from this location. The spectacular east face of Mist Mountain is beyond and to the left of Burns.

Buildings at Burns Mine
(Glenbow Archives)

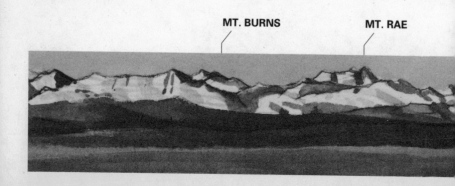

MOUNT RAE
3,225 m 82 km

The highest peak clearly identifiable from Calgary was named in honour of the great Arctic explorer, Dr. John Rae. While employed by the Hudson's Bay Company, Rae conducted four major expeditions into the uncharted Canadian Arctic, and in the course of these journeys walked the incredible distance of 36,000 km. Whereas other explorers of the era claimed that, *"the objective of polar explorations is to explore properly and not to evade the hazards of the game through the vulgar subterfuge of going native"*, John Rae adapted to the Eskimo techniques of living off the land. He was the first to bring back to England the news of Sir John Franklin's fate, although information that the expedition's members had ended their days as cannibals was not well received.

Sir James Hector, second in command of the Palliser Expedition, named the peak just four years after John Rae had reported the fate of Franklin to the world.

The fact that it was named so early in Alberta's history testifies to its prominence as the highest and northernmost summit of the Misty Range from whose slopes waters flow into the Kananaskis, Highwood, Sheep, and Elbow Rivers.

Dr. John Rae c. 1830's (Glenbow Archives)

The mountain is large in area as well as tall. Thus it appears rather block-shaped from Calgary with a distinctive notch south of the peak. It lies some 8 km beyond Cougar Mountain, while the summit of Mount Foch which can be seen to the north is a further 13 km to the west beyond the Kananaskis Lakes. Like other peaks of the Misty Range, Mount Rae is sometimes hidden in clouds when Cougar Mountain is visible. At other times the summit is covered with snow when Cougar is bare.

View to the southeast from Highway #40, 9.3 km south of the junction with Kananaskis Lakes Trail

The northern slope of the mountain contains the most easterly accumulations of glacier ice in the Rockies. During the summer and with morning sun, this glacier is often seen quite clearly from the Nose Hill vantage point. In the valley to the north lies Elbow Lake, the source of the river which flows east for 35 km before entering the foothills east of Prairie Mountain and continuing on to the City of Calgary.

The best viewpoint of the mountain's eastern cliffs is from near Pekisko on Highway #540. From this point one can look up the Sheep Valley and see the entire eastern face of Mount Rae which is most impressive. Cougar Mountain prevents all but the higher portion of the cliffs from being seen from the Nose Hill vantage point. A drive down Kananaskis Trail (#40) through Kananaskis Country to the summit of Highwood Pass takes one almost to timberline on Mount Rae's western slopes but as is often the case, the mountain is much less spectacular when viewed from the west, its broad shoulders preventing the actual summit from being seen. The only point on Highway #40 from which a good view of the actual summit can be obtained is from the approach to the steep hill leading to the top of the pass from the north side. From here one sees the darker-coloured summit rising dome-like behind the southwestern shoulder of the mountain.

The first recorded ascent of Mount Rae was made from Highwood Pass in 1950 by G. Langille and E. H. J. Smythe who had the good character to report a cairn without record on the top.

COUGAR MOUNTAIN
2,863 m 74 km

Cougars are fairly common in some areas of the eastern slopes, but because of the animal's secretive nature they are rarely seen. Many seasons can be spent in the foothills and mountains of southern Alberta without ever sighting one since by nature cougars are exceedingly alert, suspicious, and retiring. They are great travellers, ranging over 50 km from their home locality, so it is quite likely that cougars frequent the slopes of Cougar Mountain from time to time. The mountain as well as Cougar Creek which lies to the east were probably the location of some incident involving Canada's largest feline.

Like the animal, Cougar Mountain is difficult to see. A close up view from a highway is not possible, the view from the Sheep Valley being blocked by Bluerock Mountain which stands almost as high, and the view from the Elbow Valley being obstructed by the eastern ridges of Banded Peak. The mountain may be seen, however, by hiking through Elbow Pass into the Upper Elbow Valley.

The watersheds of the Sheep and Elbow Rivers are separated by a divide which lies immediately to the west of Cougar. From Sheep Lakes, the Sheep River flows south until reaching Mount Gibraltar where it turns east to the prairies, while on the opposite side of the divide, the waters flow north into the Upper Elbow River, eventually joining the Elbow near the west end of Highway #66.

Cougar Mountain from near Sheep/Elbow divide
(Photo Gillean Daffern)

FORGET-ME-NOT MOUNTAIN
2,321 m 62 km

Both mountain and ridge were named after a small but intensely blue alpine flower which grows in high alpine meadows such as those found along the top of the ridge. The true mountain Forget-Me-Not has a pure, sky-blue colour in the petals which is enhanced by a centre of rich gold and should not be confused with the False Forget-Me-Not which has paler coloured flowers and is found in moist open places from prairie elevations up to timberline.

Annora Brown, the native of Fort Macleod who became well known for her flower paintings, wrote of the plants in her book "Old Man's Garden." Noting that even the False Forget-Me-Not became a more intense blue at higher elevations, she was not terribly concerned about the confusion and wrote:

> "What matter if it be a noxious weed in the heat and drought of the prairie? In the rarer air it is both beautiful and fragrant - one of the beauties of the alpine slopes and pool's edge, worthy of all the noble sentiments that come to it from its namesake of the old world."

Alpine Forget-Me-Not

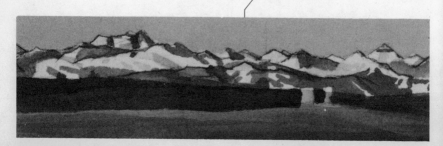

When looking at Forget-Me-Not Ridge and Mountain from Nose Hill, it is interesting to note that three other layers of mountains may be seen beyond. Banded Peak appears 11 km behind the highest point of the ridge, Elpoca Mountain (just to the right of Banded) is a further 10 km west, while to the left of Banded Peak, Mount Foch of the French Military Group may be visible a further 12 km west of Elpoca Mountain. So when looking at the mountains behind Forget-Me-Not, one is looking 33 km in all into the Rockies beyond the first peak.

The Elbow River begins 20 km southwest of Forget-Me-Not where Elbow Lake lies below the northern cliffs and glacier of Mount Rae. It flows through a valley between Banded Peak and Cougar Mountain and then turns and flows north for 11 km along the west side of Forget-Me-Not Ridge. Turning east around the north end of the ridge, it continues past the southern slopes of Prairie Mountain on its journey to Calgary and its confluence with the Bow.

On the highest point of the peak, a concrete foundation and some red-painted rocks are all that remains of the Forget-Me-Not Fire Lookout which was operated by the Alberta Forest Service from 1952 until 1975.

View to the south from the high point on Highway #66, 5.2 km west of Elbow Falls

A good viewpoint for Forget-Me-Not is from Elbow Falls Trail (#66) west of Elbow Falls. However, only the northern portion of the ridge is visible and one is too close to the mountain to appreciate its length and geographical significance.

MOUNT FOCH
3,179 m 95 km

With the exception of Mount Lyall and Mount Gass near the extreme south end of the Panorama, Mount Foch and its neighbours in the French Military Group are the only Continental Divide mountains which can be seen from Nose Hill. The group is made up of five mountains dominated by Mount Joffre, the highest point between Mount Assiniboine and the International Boundary. Barely visible even under ideal conditions, the only one of the group which can be identified with certainty is Mount Foch, the second highest peak on the Panorama.

A. O. Wheeler was a surveyor responsible for mapping many of the alpine regions of Canada. His greatest project was the survey of the interprovincial boundary between Alberta and British Columbia from the American Border to Mount Robson which involved delineating 1,000 km of the Continental Divide. While working in the southern Rockies in 1916, with patriotism at its height, Wheeler made the original suggestion that mountains in the Rockies be named after Allied military figures. He proposed that the peaks in the area of the Kananaskis Lakes be named for, *"distinguished generals who have rendered such names immortal through their splendid service to France in the great world war now in progress."*
The geographic board approved of Wheeler's idea and went even further, including British and Italian Generals as well as naval leaders and warships.

The French Military Group would have been very significant to Wheeler as a surveyor because it is at this point that the Continental Divide, which normally trends NNW-SSE, makes a ninety degree turn and for 15 km trends ENE - WSW, descending to 1,891 m as it crosses Elk Pass. This corner forms the backdrop to the Kananaskis Lakes.

Mount Foch was named after Marshall Ferdinand Foch, supreme commander of allied forces during the latter stages of the First World War. In March of 1918 a massive German offensive threatened Paris and the channel ports and it was at this point that Foch was appointed Generalissimo. Known as the Somme Offensive, it was not immediately stopped but it is thought doubtful that any other commander could have held the Allies together as he did or recovered the military initiative as quickly.

MT. FOCH

Mount Foch, which lies directly south of Upper Kananaskis Lake, may be seen from Kananaskis Trail (#40), 2.3 km south of the junction with Kananaskis Lakes Trail

Arthur Wheeler, as well as having a professional interest in travelling through the mountains, was the founder of the Alpine Club of Canada. In conjunction with a Boston professor, he originally planned on forming a "North American Alpine Club" with a Canadian branch, but when news of this reached Elizabeth Parker, a writer for the Winnipeg Free Press, she wrote an article which according to Wheeler, *"Declared my actions were unpatriotic, chided my lack of imperialism and generally gave me a penlashing...."*. Wheeler then called upon Miss Parker for assistance in forming a purely Canadian organization and the two were the driving force behind the formation of the Alpine Club of Canada.

Mount Joffre was first climbed by Katie Gardiner with guide Walter Feuz who, like most of the early alpine guides in the Rockies, did not enjoy working for the somewhat militaristic President Wheeler of the Alpine Club. Feuz felt that Arthur Wheeler was *"too bossy"* and most of the other guides agreed.

Arthur Wheeler in 1913 (Glenbow Archives)

BANDED PEAK
2,934 m 73 km

During winter months, Banded Peak is one of the easiest mountains to identify from Calgary. In outline the peak is perfectly triangular with a horizontal band of black just below the summit caused by a steep cliff about 30 m high. The rock layer which forms the band is dark in colour, resulting in the band being somewhat noticeable even in summer.

Banded Peak is the southernmost of a very prominent group of front range mountains. Together with Mounts Glasgow, Cornwall, and an unnamed peak between Cornwall and Banded Peak, the group occupies the area between the Elbow River which passes to the south of Banded Peak, and the Little Elbow River which flows below the northern slopes of Mount Glasgow. For some reason, this group is prone to receiving snowfalls in the late spring, early fall, and even summer when the surrounding mountains, some of them significantly higher, do not receive any snow at all.

The unnamed mountain situated between Banded Peak and Mount Cornwall is equal in height to Mount Cornwall and slightly higher than Banded Peak. It too exhibits a band near the summit, although it is not as clearly defined as that on Banded Peak. It is difficult to understand why it was ignored in 1922 when other mountains in this small range were named in honour of warships belonging to the Royal Navy.

View to the southwest from the bottom of the big hill, 7.6 km west of Elbow Falls on Highway #66

The best viewpoint for a close look at Banded Peak is from Elbow Falls Trail (#66) near the junction of the Elbow and Little Elbow Rivers. Mount Glasgow is visible as well, but the summits of Mount Cornwall and the unnamed peak are hidden behind high ridges. From this point, Banded Peak is viewed from the same angle as from Nose Hill and so the silhouette and band appear very similar but much larger.

BANDED PEAK

ELPOCA MOUNTAIN
3,033 m 83 km

George Pocaterra (left) with Spotted Wolf (Glenbow Archives)

The mountain was named for George Pocaterra who travelled extensively in the Kananaskis-Highwood area during the early 1900's. Born in a valley of the Italian Alps, he was well educated and could speak five languages. After coming to Canada as a young man, he established the famous Buffalo Head Ranch in the Highwood Valley which was eventually purchased by close friend Raymond Patterson.

As well as ranching, Pocaterra was involved in trapping, hunting, coal exploration and in the general exploration of the area. Some of the trips undertaken with Raymond Patterson are described in Patterson's best known book "The Buffalo Head".

While becoming familiar with many untravelled areas in southern Alberta, Pocaterra made friends with the Indians. He was very proud of learning their native languages and folklore, and became blood brother to a Stoney named Spotted Wolf, travelling with him into the wild country of the Rockies when the only access was via ancient Indian trails.

The country that George Pocaterra loved changed extensively with the development of the Kananaskis Valley to produce electrical power. Pocaterra wrote, *"I was probably the first white man to see the beautiful lake district from the south. The most beautiful mountain scenery in the world, as far as I am concerned, was at these lakes, but now it is completely spoiled by the power dams, and the drowning of the marvelously beautiful islands and exquisitely curving beaches, the cutting down of the century old trees, and the drying up of the twin falls between the two lakes and of the falls below the lower lake."*

Schooner Island, one of Pocaterra's "marvelously beautiful islands" (Glenbow Archives)

Elpoca Mountain is the southernmost peak of the Opal Range and the only one not named after a British Naval Commander involved in the Battle of Jutland during the First World War. It lies 6 km to the east of Lower Kananaskis Lake and immediately north of Elbow Lake. From the Nose Hill vantage point it appears on the Panorama just to the right of but actually 10 km beyond the easily recognizable Banded Peak. It is a difficult mountain to climb, the first recorded ascent not being made until 1960 according to mountaineering records.

Elpoca Mountain is very prominent as one drives north from Highwood Pass on Kananaskis Trail (#40). This view is somewhat deceptive in that the southern peak, which does not appear challenging, appears higher than the more distant portion of the mountain. In fact, the northern peak is 250 m higher than the southern peak.

View to the north-northwest from Highway #40, 4.1 km north of the summit of Highwood Pass

The valley to the east of Elpoca Mountain contains Piper Creek although the name has yet to be officially recognized. Norma Piper, a coloratura soprano very active in the Calgary operatic community, became George Pocaterra's wife in 1936. Evidence of the breadth of George Pocaterra's interests is the fact that he acted as stage manager for the operatic company with which she sang.

TOMBSTONE MOUNTAIN
3,033 m 78 km

George Dawson, one of the most outstanding scientists Canada has ever produced, named Tombstone Mountain for the gravestone-like slabs of rock near the summit. Known as "Doctor George", he was Assistant Director of the Geologic Survey of Canada in 1883 and 1884 when conducting the first survey by the Government of Canada in the mountains west of Calgary, all previous work having been done by the CPR. His task was to establish the courses of the major rivers and the locations of the main peaks and passes.

George Dawson had a reputation for excellence, his maps being referred to as *"a literal photograph of the country containing information phenomenally complete and accurate."* This quality of work was a result of tremendous physical effort in the field despite his short stature complicated by a chronic chest weakness and a back humped by a childhood accident. He was described as having a *"cheerful, amiable disposition, combined with an indomitable will and an insatiable passion for exploration and discovery."*

George Dawson in 1885 (National Archives of Canada)

Despite an elevation in excess of 3,000 m, Tombstone is one of four mountains making up the Panorama from Nose Hill that cannot be seen from relatively close range without going hiking. A walk through Elbow Pass from Kananaskis Trail (#40) to just beyond Elbow Lake is the easiest way to get a look at the mountain which appears almost directly north as one looks down the upper Elbow River Valley.

Although he was appointed director of the Geologic Survey of Canada in 1895, Dawson's interests and studies extended beyond geology into many other fields of science. His field journal even contained the occasional poem including this one with a geological flavour:

Contorted bed, of unknown age,
  My weary limbs shall bear,
Perhaps a neat synclinal fold
  At night shall be my lair.
Dips I shall take in unnamed streams,
  Or where the rocks strike, follow
Along the crested mountain ridge
  Or anticlinal hollow...
Where long neglected mountains stand
  Just crumbling into shreds
And laying bare on every hand
  The treasures of their beds.

MOUNTS CORNWALL & GLASGOW
2,956 m 73 km & 2,950 m 71 km

HMS Glasgow

    Mounts Cornwall and Glasgow are two of over a dozen peaks in Kananaskis Country named after British warships of World War I. Most were ships which participated in the Battle of Jutland in 1916, but HMS Cornwall and Glasgow were both cruisers which played a significant role in the 1914 Battle of the Falkland Islands.

    The Cornwall and Glasgow, together with HMS Kent, were pursuing three German warships trying to escape the main battle and seek refuge in Tierra del Fuego. Choosing to concentrate their attention on the German light cruiser Leipzig, HMS Glasgow engaged first, attempting to slow down the fleeing German ship and allow the Cornwall to catch up and assist. The Glasgow suffered some hits but soon HMS Cornwall came in range and as its captain wrote, *"Cornwall hit the Leipzig's foretopmast and carried it away, turned to starboard and I poured in my whole broadside"*. The two English ships then engaged their wounded quarry from opposite sides, their fire becoming more and more effective as they slowly closed the range. Out of ammunition, the Leipzig fired its last two torpedoes but the British had by then retreated out of range. They then re-approached the Leipzig to see if the Germans had *"struck her colours"*, but since her ensign was still flying, opened fire once more. Her flag still flying, the Leipzig heeled over to sink rapidly by her bows. The British ships could rescue only 18 of the 286 sailors and Capt. Ellerton of HMS Cornwall, *"regretted that an officer as gallant as Captain Haun of the Leipzig was not one of them"*.

The most distinguishing characteristic of Mount Cornwall is the "Cornwall Snowpatch". This circular shaped area of snow just below the summit often lasts throughout the entire summer and by late August of most years is the only snow remaining visible from Calgary with the exception of the glacier on the north slope of Mount Rae.

The mountain lies 2 km to the southwest of Mount Glasgow. When views of Mount Glasgow and Banded Peak appear from Elbow Falls Trail (#66) near Forget-Me-Not Ridge, Mount Cornwall is hidden behind the east ridge of Mount Glasgow. In fact, a close-up view of Mount Cornwall is not available from any highway. The best viewpoint is from west of Millarville on Highway #549.

View to the west from Highway #549, 3.3 km west of the junction with Highway #22 of Mount Cornwall (centre) and Mount Glasgow (right)

The first recorded ascent of both mountains was by Arnold Choquette of Calgary who made solo ascents on skis in May of 1949.

Mount Glasgow lies just to the north of Mount Cornwall on the Panorama, the two standing side-by-side on the horizon just as their namesakes did in the Battle of the Falkland Islands.

The ship's armament consisted of two 6 inch guns (one fore and aft), ten 4 inch guns (five along each side) and two submerged torpedo tubes. 430 feet long, she carried up to 750 tons of coal to fire the boilers which were capable of generating 22,000 horse-power and a speed of 26 knots. 376 sailors were required to man the ship.

Most of the major streets in Calgary run north-south or east-west. However, Richmond Road in southwest Calgary is oriented perpendicular to the trend of the mountain panorama and when one is travelling in a southwesterly direction on this thoroughfare on a clear day, it is difficult not to notice Mount Glasgow. It is the very prominent, pyramid-shaped peak with large, smooth areas on the faces of the pyramid which often form completely white, unbroken snow slopes.

Although the mountain looks very high and spectacular from the junction of the Elbow and Little Elbow Rivers at the end of Elbow Falls Trail (#66), the beautiful pyramid shape is not apparent from this point and there is little resemblance to the view from Richmond Road or Nose Hill.

View of Mount Glasgow looking southwest from the bottom of the big hill, 7.6 km west of Elbow Falls on Highway #66

MT. GLASGOW   **MT. BLANE**

MOUNT BLANE
2,972 m 81 km

Like most mountains of the Opal Range, Mount Blane is quite spectacular. On the Panorama it is a rather sharp, symmetric peak with a distinctive notch on the south ridge and vertical cliffs facing both the prairies and the Kananaskis Valley. The first ascents of all of the peaks in the range were made in the 1950's, an indication of their challenge from a mountaineering point of view.

According to the official records of the Governments of Canada and Alberta, Mount Blane was named after Sir C. R. Blane, commander of the battle-cruiser HMS Queen Mary in the Battle of Jutland. However, the records of the Battle of Jutland indicate that C. I. Prowse was the commander of the Queen Mary and no mention is made of a C. R. Blane. Although it is known that Blane died at the Battle of Jutland, whether or not he was aboard the Queen Mary is not known. If he was, we do not know why he and not Prowse was chosen to be honoured in this way.

Mount Blane is the southernmost of seven peaks in the Opal Range named in honour of British naval commanders involved in the Battle of Jutland which was the major naval confrontation between the British and Germans during the First World War. The German navy was facing the greatest battle fleet the world had ever seen when it challenged the Royal Navy in 1916. When the smoke had cleared the British had lost six cruisers and eight destroyers while the Germans had lost one battleship, five cruisers and five destroyers.

The tactical victory is said to have gone to the Germans as they had inflicted double their own losses in terms of tonnage against a greatly superior opponent. In addition, the British lost over twice as many men as the Germans. However, the German fleet was forced to retreat and never again ventured forth from its protected harbour of Helgoland. Thus, it is argued, the British were victorious as Britannia continued to rule the waves for the duration of the Great War. At any rate, this great battle at sea did little to change the ratio of strength between the two fleets or the strategic situation in the war.

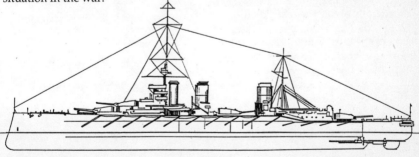

HMS Queen Mary

The HMS Queen Mary was a Royal Navy battlecruiser. Although more lightly armoured than battleships, battlecruisers often exceeded them in size and the Queen Mary was one of the largest warships in the British fleet. *"About 16:26 she met her doom"* from the concentrated fire of two German ships, the Derfflinger and the Seydlitz. Her final moments were described by Von Hase of the Derfflinger, *"First of all a vivid red flame shot up from her forepart. Then came an explosion forward which was followed by a much heavier explosion amidships. Black debris flew into the air and immediately afterwards the whole ship blew up with a terrific explosion; a gigantic cloud of smoke rose, the masts collapsed inwards and the smoke hid everything."* An officer aboard HMS New Zealand reported, *"We passed the Queen Mary about 150 yards on our port beam, by which time the smoke had blown clear, revealing the stern from the funnel aft afloat and the propellers still revolving, but the forward part had already gone under. When we were abreast, this after portion rolled over and blew up. Great masses of iron were thrown into the air and things were falling into the sea round us. Before we had quite passed, the Queen Mary completely disappeared."* Of the crew of 1275, all but 7 were killed.

Because a very high ridge rises immediately above the east side of Kananaskis Trail (#40), most of the peaks of the Opal Range are difficult to see except where steep-walled valleys cut through the ridge. Mount Blane can be spotted through the valley formed by King Creek.

View to the east-northeast from the junction of Highway #40 and the Kananaskis Lakes Trail

MOUNT BROCK
2,879 m 81 km

View to the northeast from the junction of the Smith-Dorrien Road and the Kananaskis Lakes Trail

Mount Brock is most impressive from Peter Lougheed Provincial Park near the Interpretive Centre on the road leading to Kananaskis Lakes. Like Mount Blane, it is quite symmetric but has two small notches, one on the north ridge and one on the south.

In profile on the Panorama, Mount Brock closely resembles Mount Blane. The mountains are quite similar from all angles and are also related in that Rear Admiral O. Brock was commander of the First Battlecruiser Squadron which included Commander Blane's HMS Queen Mary.

The Opal Range was named by George Dawson after he discovered many small cavities lined with quartz and coated with thin films of opal. The vertical dipping beds which characterize the mountain and the entire Opal Range are layers of limestone which were once horizontal, having been deposited at the bottom of the sea in Mississippian Time 325 million years ago. They are of the Rundle Formation and are, in fact, the same layer which forms the upper cliffs of Mount Rundle.

Opal Range from Fortress Mountain ski area (Photo Gillean Daffern)

MOUNT HOOD
2,873 m 80 km

Rear Admiral H. L. A. Hood led the Third Battlecruiser Squadron into the Battle of Jutland. The squadron, made up of HMS Invincible, Hood's flagship, as well as HMS Indomitable and HMS Inflexible, was in action against German battleships including the Derfflinger, the ship that sunk the Queen Mary. An officer watching the battle from another ship recalled, *"Rear Admiral Hood pressed home his attack, and it was an inspiring sight to see this squadron of battle cruisers dashing towards the enemy with every gun in action."* Initially, Hood's battlecruisers were successful in landing some heavy blows on enemy ships and Hood encouraged his gunnery officers, *"Your fire is very good. Keep at it as quickly as you can. Every shot is telling."*

But suddenly, the ever-shifting low cloud and mist began to favour the enemy and German shells began to strike the Invincible. *"Flames shot up from the gallant flagship and there came again the awful spectacle of a fiery burst, followed by a huge column of dark smoke which, mottled with blackened debris, swelled up hundreds of feet in the air, and the mother of all battle cruisers had gone"*. The North Sea is relatively shallow where the Invincible was struck with the result that the ship created her own tombstones for her 1,026 dead which included the Rear Admiral. *"She blew up exactly in half. The two ends then subsided, resting on the bottom, so that they stood up almost vertically with the stem and stern standing an appreciable distance out of the water"*.

HMS Invincible broken in half and resting on the sea-bed.

View to the east from the Hood Creek Bridge on Highway #40, 3.4 km north of the junction with Kananaskis Lakes Trail

Mount Hood, a peak of the Opal Range, is visible from Kananaskis Trail (#40) through the valley made by Hood Creek as it flows east into the Kananaskis River. The peak to the left is Mount Packenham, probably the most spectacular of the Opals but not visible from Nose Hill.

From the summit of Hood, mountains honouring two of the other three battlecruisers may be seen. Mount Invincible lies near the southern end of the Spray Range to the west of Lower Kananaskis Lakes, while Mount Inflexible - a peak of the Kananaskis Range - lies directly across the Kananaskis Valley from the mountain named in honour of the Rear Admiral who commanded the squadron. For some reason, the name of HMS Indomitable was not given to a mountain.

MT. HOOD

MOUNTS ROMULUS AND REMUS
2,831 m 73 km & 2,688 m 71 km

When snow conditions are optimum, Mount Romulus is one of the most distinctive and easily recognized mountains seen from Calgary. It is somewhat block shaped with a flat top and steep cliffs to the east and southeast. In winter, prevailing westerly and northwesterly winds create a large horizontal cornice of snow along the cliff top which faces the prairies. When most of the snow has melted off the nearby mountains, this long cornice is very noticeable.

Although Mount Remus does not form part of the skyline from Nose Hill, with suitable lighting conditions it can be seen in front of the higher and more distant Mount Romulus. Both mountains lie to the northwest of Mount Glasgow, across the valley of the Little Elbow River.

View to the west from the Little Elbow Campground at the western end of Highway #66

Romulus and Remus were the legendary founders of Rome. Twin sons of Mars and Rhea Silvia, they were abandoned and cast adrift on the Tiber, ultimately washing ashore where they were suckled by a wolf and fed by a woodpecker. They were then adopted by a shepherd and later founded the city that was to become Rome. Romulus surrounded it with a wall, but Remus in contempt jumped over it so Romulus killed him and reigned alone in the city which was named for him.

Just as in the Roman legend, Mount Romulus dominates Mount Remus which lies just to its east but is some 150 m lower in elevation.

A closer view of Romulus and Remus may be obtained from the Little Elbow campground located at the end of Elbow Falls Trail (#66). From this point, Mount Remus appears to be significantly higher than Romulus. However, this is merely illusion due to the proximity of the viewpoint and the fact that Mount Romulus lies 1.5 km farther to the southwest.

MOUNT EVAN-THOMAS
2,941 m 79 km

Although only the highest part of Mount Evan-Thomas appears above the Fisher Range from Nose Hill, the mountain can look quite spectacular under optimum lighting and snow conditions. It is the northernmost named peak of the Opals, although the range continues for another 7 km. In all, the Opal Range stretches for 22 km from Rocky Creek, 5 km north of Fortress Mountain Turnoff, to the Elbow River beyond Elpoca Mountain.

From Kananaskis Trail (#40), only a fleeting glimpse of Evan-Thomas is possible through a small valley just to the north of Hood Creek.

The peak is named after Rear Admiral H. Evan-Thomas who commanded the Fifth Battle CruiserSquadron at the Battle of Jutland in 1916

View to the northeast from Highway #40, 0.7 km north of the Hood Creek Bridge

MT. ROMULUS   MT. EVAN-THOMAS

FISHER PEAK
3,052 m 73 km

View to the southeast from the Evan-Thomas Creek Bridge on Highway #40, 4.8 km south of the Nakiska access road

Fisher Peak appears very high on the Panorama with its south and north ridges forming the skyline for a considerable distance. Two hundred and twenty metres taller than any other peak in the group, it completely dominates the Fisher Range which lies east of Kananaskis Trail (#40) and stretches from Barrier Lake in the north to the Little Elbow River in the south.

As was the case with many of the more prominent mountains, Fisher Peak was named by the Palliser Expedition, in this case by Captain John Palliser himself after one of his companions on a hunting expedition to Louisiana in 1847.

A good viewpoint for Fisher Peak is from Evan-Thomas Creek bridge on Kananaskis Trail (#40). From here one looks southeast up the headwaters of Evan-Thomas Creek to where Fisher Peak stands in the distance 11 km away.

The mountain is also visible from Mount Romulus backcountry campground at the western end of Elbow Falls Trail (#66). From this point, a broad cliffband rising to the east near the summit characterizes the mountain when viewed from the southeast and is especially noticeable when highlighted by snow.

PRAIRIE MOUNTAIN
2,205 m 56 km

Prairie Mountain is a small peak lying 2 km to the south of the much more massive Moose Mountain. The two are divided by Canyon Creek.

The lowest peak identified on the Panorama, Prairie Mountain has a grassy summit with trees reaching very nearly to the top. It is named after the creek to the southwest which has patches of prairie near Powderface Trail.

It is easily identifiable from Elbow Falls Trail (#66) which crosses the south slopes of the mountain on its way to the foot of Mount Glasgow.

View to the west-southwest from just east of the Elbow River Bridge on Highway #66, 9.3 km west of the junction with Highway #22

FISHER PEAK   PRAIRIE MTN.

NIHAHI RIDGE
2,545 m 65 km

The ridge lies east of the main front range and stretches from the Elbow River north to the headwaters of Prairie Creek. With an elevation of only 2,545 m, Nihahi Ridge is one of the lower features identifiable from Calgary. What makes it fairly easy to locate on the Panorama is its length of 8 km and the not very high but very long cliff along the eastern side of the ridge. If the cornice on Mount Romulus is present it can be used as a guide since Romulus, although 8 km beyond Nihahi Ridge, occurs on the Panorama between the ridge's southern end and midpoint.

The southern portion of this long ridge may be viewed from the west end of Elbow Falls Trail (#66). However, from close up the east facing cliffs are somewhat disappointing as they are neither as high nor as near vertical as they appear with morning light from Nose Hill.

The name Nihahi is the Stoney Indian word meaning "rocky" and probably refers to the very noticeable cliffband visible from the east.

View to the northwest from near Forget-Me-Not Pond at the western end of Highway #66

NIHAHI RIDGE   **MT. HOWARD**

MOUNT HOWARD
2,777 m 69 km

Ted Howard, after whom the mountain was named in 1939, was born in Pakistan, the son of a British Army Officer. He came to the foothills country in 1898 and rode for many of the early ranchers between the Sheep River and Willow Creek. Upon his return from World War I, he became the Elbow District Forest Ranger and spent the next twenty years based at Bragg Creek Ranger Station where he gained the respect of all for his honesty, kindness, and the hard work he did for the Alberta Forest Service.

Ted Howard (courtesy Millarville Historical Society)

Although it is an attractive feature on the Panorama from Nose Hill, Mount Howard is one of the lesser peaks of the Fisher Range. It lies between Nihahi Ridge to the east and the highest member of the Fisher Range, Fisher Peak, to the west.

Mount Howard is one of four peaks on the Panorama which cannot be viewed from a nearby highway. It is not a high mountain and Powderface Ridge and Nihahi Ridge combine to block the view from Elbow Falls Trail (#66), while from the other direction the main portion of the Fisher Range obstructs any view from Kananaskis Trail (#40). A hike along the Nihahi Ridge Trail to the higher portion of the ridge is one way of viewing this attractive peak at the headwaters of Nihahi Creek.

MOOSE MOUNTAIN
2,473 m 55 km

Moose Mountain is the closest mountain to Calgary by 14 km. This fact, combined with the mountain's length in a north-south direction of over 6 km results in it taking up a much longer portion of the Panorama than any other mountain. Its various ridges and minor summits occupy all of the view from Mount Howard to Mount McDougall. At 2,473 m it is one of the lowest mountains on the Panorama, but again, because it is so much closer than the others, it is very prominent especially when mountains to the west are obscured by storms restricting views to Moose Mountain alone.

The peak is located north of the Elbow River and 19 km directly west of Bragg Creek. Because of its location significantly east of the main front range, Moose Mountain was a natural choice for an Alberta Forest Service fire lookout when the system was established in 1929. The current building was built in 1974 and is the third to occupy the site.

*Moose Mountain Lookout
(Photo Gillean Daffern)*

*View to the west from the top of the hill on Highway #22,
16.2 km west of the junction with #22X*

The view of Moose Mountain from Highway #22 just east of the junction with Elbow Falls Trail (#66) illustrates the mountains areal extent with long horizontal ridges stretching north and south from the smoothly-curved summit. Another good viewpoint is from the top of the high hill on the Trans-Canada Highway near the eastern entrance to the Stoney Indian Reserve. This view to the south illustrates Moose Mountain's aloofness from the main trend of the front ranges.

The Moose Mountain Dome is a major geological structure which caused this mountain to rise up to the east of the main trend of the front ranges. It was also responsible for the creation of the Moose Mountain gas field to the east of the mountain.

All the front range mountains of the southern Alberta Rockies were formed by thrust faulting. However, in the case of Moose Mountain several thrust faults have occurred in close proximity to one another, resulting in a stacking of Paleozoic layers. A well drilled from the summit of the peak would encounter the top of the Paleozoic layer five times before finally reaching the Pre-Cambrian.

An extensive cave system lies within the southern portion of the mountain. Called the Bragg Creek Ice Cave, its slit-shaped entrance is located at the base of a cliff band above Canyon Creek. So far, experienced and well-equipped spelunkers have mapped 494 m of passageways.

Ice Cave entrance
(Photo Gillean Daffern)

MOOSE MTN.

MOUNT McDOUGALL
2,728 m 72 km

The mountain was named in honour of Reverend George McDougall and his sons who are chiefly remembered as early missionaries among the Stoneys. Initially, George McDougall established a mission near Edmonton in 1862 and there worked tirelessly among the Crees and Blackfoot of the area converting many to Christianity. In 1869 tragedy struck in the form of a smallpox epidemic introduced by the non-natives and as the McDougalls watched helplessly, thousands of Indians without immunity died, many in close proximity to the missions.

Four years later, the McDougalls went among the Stoneys and established the mission at Morley in a temporary church covered with birch bark which in later years was replaced by a wooden church known today as the Morley Memorial church. The mission quickly developed into a village of 500 people with a school, orphanage, and trading post. From the beginning the Stoneys had loved and trusted the McDougalls so it was a sad day for them when George McDougall lost his life in a raging blizzard while on a buffalo hunt in 1876. His son John carried on the work after his father's death.

View to the northeast from Highway #40, 0.6 km south of Wedge Pond

Rev. George McDougall (Glenbow Archives)

From the Nose Hill vantage point, Mount McDougall appears just to the right of Moose Mountain. An indication of Moose Mountain's distance from the front ranges is the fact that McDougall lies 17 km beyond Moose, and Mount Kidd, just to the right of McDougall, lies a further 10 km beyond McDougall.

McDougall is situated to the east of Kananaskis Trail (#40) between Wasootch Creek to the north and Evan-Thomas Creek to the south and is not particularly spectacular from any viewpoint on the highway. Smoothly-contoured, it covers a large area and is made up of many minor summits all of which are lower than neighbouring peaks to the west.

A good viewpoint for Mount McDougall is from the vicinity of Wedge Pond on Kananaskis Trail (#40).

MOUNT KIDD
2,958 m 82 km

View to the northwest rom the Rocky Creek Bridge on Highway #40

Mount Kidd is the "Pilot Mountain" of the Kananaskis Valley. Surveyor George Dawson named Pilot Mountain in Banff National Park for its location on the outside of a major bend in the Bow Valley which made the peak visible for long distances up and down the valley. Mount Kidd is similarly situated, being visible from both the northern entrance of the Kananaskis Valley near the Trans-Canada Highway and from the Kananaskis Lakes area to the south.

Occupying an area between Galatea Creek to the south and Ribbon Creek to the north, Mount Kidd is a massive mountain of which only a small portion can be seen on the Panorama just to the right of easily-recognizable Mount Bogart. The northernmost top is the highest of two summits about 2.5 km apart. Located between the mountain and Kananaskis Trail (#40) are two world class golf courses designed by Robert Trent Jones.

The massive character of the mountain as well as its two separate peaks are best seen from the vicinity of Rocky Creek on Kananaskis Trail (#40). Looking most impressive from this viewpoint are highly contorted layers of limestone which form the southwestern face of the south summit and guide a waterfall down from the highest levels to the scree slopes below. These layers mark the northern limit of the Lewis Thrust Fault, a major geologic feature which was involved in the formation of the Opal Range south of Mount Kidd, and of the Elk and High Rock Ranges as well which form the Great Divide from Kananaskis Lakes to the Crowsnest Pass.

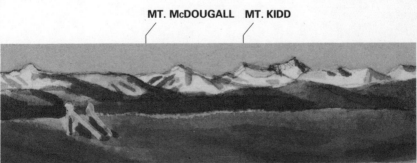

Stuart Kidd (left) with Con "Dutch" Bernhard, packer and guide to Martin Nordegg c. 1920 (Glenbow Archives)

Stuart Kidd originally lived near Calgary but according to his son could not resist the attraction of the mountains and so moved to Morley in 1907 where he operated the Scott and Leeson Trading Post. Kidd became fluent in the Stoney language and was made an honourary chief, probably the first white to be so honoured, and given the name of "Tah-Osa" which means "Moose Killer". Part of his job was outfitting survey parties which worked in the Kananaskis Valley area. One of these was led by a geologist D. Bogart Dowling who chose Kidd's name for the most impressive mountain in the valley.

Mount Kidd Loookout below cliffs of the northernmost top (Photo Gillean Daffern)

Mount Kidd Fire Lookout can be seen on the high ridge below the steep cliffs of the north face. Constructed in 1981, it is the most recent addition to the series of fire lookouts established in the late 1920's and stands guard over the Province's significant financial interests in the valley below: the golf course, the ski resort development, and the hotels.

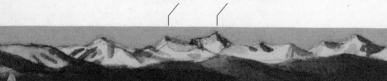

MOUNT BOGART
3,144 m 84 km

Mount Bogart, the highest peak in the range lying between the Kananaskis and Spray Lakes Valleys, is separated from Mount Kidd by Ribbon Creek which flows to the south of it. Although it is not significantly higher than its neighbours to the north - Mounts Sparrowhawk, Wind, and Lougheed - the snow seems to linger on its summit longer and the mountain is often quite noticeable for this reason. It also seems somewhat aloof from nearby peaks and these factors as well as its height makes it one of the more easily recognizable points on the Panorama.

Although almost 200 m higher than Mount Kidd, Bogart is hidden from view by Kidd and other peaks as one approaches the mountain from the south along Kananaskis Trail (#40). However, when driving up the valley from the north, one gets a fine view of the mountain looming 700 m above the highest ski slopes of Mount Allan.

Mount Bogart was named in 1904 in honour of Dr. D. Bogart Dowling, a geologist who pioneered in the areas of coal and petroleum geology in Canada. It is the fourth highest peak identifiable from Calgary and together with the second highest, Mount Foch, was first climbed by a lady.

View to the southwest from the Porcupine Creek Bridge on Highway #40, 9.8 km south of the Kananaskis Country Information Centre

Walter Feuz

Katie Gardiner (Whyte Museum of the Canadian Rockies) She made more first ascents in the Canadian Rockies than any other woman, and only three men other than professional guides exceeded her total of thirty-three.

Katherine (Katie) Gardiner arrived for her first season of climbing in the Canadian Rockies in 1929, travelling alone on the CPR. However, she was no stranger to climbing and exploration. The daughter of a distinguished British climber who was the first to reach the summit of Mount Elbruz, she had often accompanied him on his annual climbing trip to the Alps. Upon her arrival in Banff, she contacted Walter Feuz, the youngest of a family of alpine guides brought over from Switzerland by the CPR and together with two packers they explored the country between the Bow Valley and the Crowsnest Pass.

Impressed by the guiding services of Feuz as well as finding the area to her liking (particularly the opportunity for first ascents), she returned the next two seasons as well. Always accompanied by Feuz, she completed a total of 14 first ascents in the area including Mount Bogart in 1930.

Ken Jones, who has been a guide in the Rockies since the 1930's and currently resides in Nanton, remembers meeting Katie at Shadow Lake in Banff National Park. He was to lead Miss Gardiner and two friends on an ascent of Mount Ball and initially wondered what he had gotten himself in for as his client was very clumsy on the trail and looked *"as though she could trip over her own shadow"*. To Ken's relief, however, she was very capable when the trail was left behind and the rock climbing began.

In subsequent years, Kate continued climbing in Canada, visiting the spectacular Bugaboo area of the Purcell Range in 1935 with Ken Jones and Walter Perren. When in their fifties, Katie and guides Edward Feuz and Christian Häsler climbed Mount Robson, the highest peak in the Rockies and considered a very difficult ascent. Upon their return to Lake Louise when it was suggested that it must have been a tough climb, Ed Feuz replied, *"Hard?, Why with Katie Gardiner along, it was a piece of cake."*

MOUNT SPARROWHAWK
3,121 m 84 km

View to the west-northwest from Highway #40, 1.7 km south of the Nakiska access road

The mountain is located directly west of the Nakiska access road and the old coal mine on Mount Allan. From Kananaskis Trail (#40) the view is limited to a very short stretch just south of the Nakiska access road junction. There is an interesting but fairly distant view of the mountain from the Trans-Canada Highway just east of the Banff National Park Gates where Mount Sparrowhawk appears beyond and to the right of Mount Lougheed.

Mount Sparrowhawk, together with Wind Mountain, a minor peak north of Wind, and the twin summits of Mount Lougheed form a series of five sharp, high peaks which appear quite close together on the Panorama. A distinguishing feature is a large cornice of snow which lies in the col just to the south of the mountain until very late in the summer.

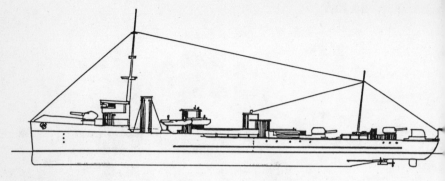

HMS *Sparrowhawk*

One might expect that this mountain would have been named after the small falcon which is a common summer resident of our province. It was, however, named after HMS Sparrowhawk, a Royal Navy destroyer sunk during the Battle of Jutland in World War I.

Although the crew performed valiantly, Sparrowhawk's role in the Battle of Jutland was not one to bring fame and honour to the Royal Navy. She was one of a flotilla of some eleven destroyers proceeding through a very dark night with absolutely no idea of where the enemy was and with only a very vague idea of the position of other British ships. In the course of the battle, the destroyers turned to fire torpedoes and as a crew member of the Sparrowhawk related, *"the helm was put over and orders passed to fire the remaining torpedo. The HMS Broke, ahead of us, had also put her helm over but, just as we were both turning, she was hit forward, and when she should have eased her helm and steadied to fire a torpedo, as we were doing, I saw that she was still swinging to port with her helm jammed, and coming straight for our bridge at 28 knots. I remember shouting a warning to everyone to hold on, and to the forward gun's crew to clear the forecastle, just as she hit us."*

HMS Contest, following in the night, failed to see the damaged Sparrowhawk and sliced off her stern, leaving the crippled Sparrowhawk to lie where she was, unable to steam. At dawn, the Sparrowhawk's crew was horrified when a German light cruiser appeared. Bravely they prepared to engage the much larger enemy warship with their only remaining operable gun while dead in the water. Much to their relief the enemy ship did not open fire, but *"settled down forward, then stood on her head and sank"*. She was the Ebling which had been severely damaged in an earlier engagement and had been trying to reach the Danish coast. An hour later HMS Marksman appeared and took the Sparrowhawk in tow, but when both hawsers broke, the unfortunate Sparrowhawk was ordered sunk by British gunfire.

WIND MOUNTAIN
3,124 m 82 km

Wind Mountain, together with Mount Sparrowhawk to the south and the twin summits of Mount Lougheed to the north form a unique set of contiguous peaks on the Panorama in that they all appear within 2 km of each other in distance from Nose Hill and in addition, are within 43 m of each other in elevation. Thus they appear to be almost exactly the same height when viewed from Calgary.

The history and background of what is now known as Wind Mountain is difficult to separate from that of its neighbor Mount Lougheed.

Please refer to Mount Lougheed for additional information.

View to the northwest from Highway #40, 2.6 km south of the Nakiska access road

When travelling along Kananaskis Trail (#40) just north of the Nakiska access road, one gets a brief glimpse of this impressive tower-shaped peak between the slopes of Mount Kidd and Mount Allan. The mountain is also visible from the Trans-Canada Highway near Dead Man Flat where it presents the same profile.

WIND MTN.

MOUNT ALLAN
2,819 m 81 km

Mount Allan is a small, rather unspectacular mountain which has considerable recent history. Although it does not quite reach the skyline on the Panorama, it can be seen just below the col to the north of Wind Mountain. It lies 3 km closer to Calgary than Mounts Sparrowhawk, Wind, and Lougheed which form part of the range separating the Kananaskis Valley from the Spray Lakes Valley to the west.

Dr. J. A. Allan, who in 1912 became the first professor of geology at the University of Alberta, was responsible for recording much of the coal reserves in Alberta. When driving down Kananaskis Trail (#40), one can spot the reclaimed scar of an abandoned coal mine on the slopes of the mountain named after Dr. Allan in 1948.

Coal in Alberta is found in rocks of the Mesozoic Era. In fact, Mount Allan is entirely made up of rocks of this era which explains its smooth, rounded slopes. The Kananaskis Exploration and Development Company began operating the coal mine in 1947, operating it initially as a strip mine but later developing it into an underground mine complete with a railway and cars. In 1948 their families came to join the mine workers and a number of tarpaper shacks and log cabins were built below the mine on the north bank of Ribbon Creek. As the village grew to a population of almost two hundred people, it was given the name Kovach after Joe Kovach the District Forest Ranger.

Slumping coal markets forced the closure of the mine in 1952 and today only some crumbling stone work and foundations remain in the forest which has overgrown the old townsite. On the mountainside, the mine scar appears as a lush meadow and is a good example of reclamation.

MT. ALLAN

View to the west-northwest from the Kananaskis River Bridge on the Nakiska access road, just west of Highway #40

A more interesting view is not from the Kananaskis Valley at all but from Dead Man Flat on the Trans-Canada Highway. Looking southeast from this location one views the long, straight, north ridge rising to the summit which from this direction appears left of the higher and much more spectacular Mount Lougheed.

School house at Kovach, 1962 (Glenbow Archives)

Mount Allan was, of course, the controversial site of alpine skiing events during the 1988 Olympic Winter Games. The Alpine Village development nearby is touted to be a world class facility and is in striking contrast to the old village of Kovach, or as it was more popularly known *"The Camp on Ribbon Crick"*.

In 1966 the Rocky Mountain Ramblers, a Calgary based hiking group, decided to build a trail from the old townsite to the summit and on down the long north ridge to Dead Man Flat on the Trans-Canada Highway. It was the organization's Centennial Project and when finished became the highest maintained trail in the Canadian Rockies.

MOUNT LOUGHEED
3,107 m 84 km

Eugene Bourgeau was the botanist on the Palliser Expedition of 1857-1860, his career having begun with his love of flowers in the French Alps where he tended his father's herds. Captain Palliser wrote that Bourgeau, *"was a great favourite with us all. In addition to his acquirements as a botanist, he united the most sociable jovial disposition, ever ready not only to do his own work, but assist anyone else who asked him."*.

On the day Bourgeau first saw the mountain while travelling up the Bow Valley in 1858, clouds were swirling around the summit and so he named it Wind Mountain. He later ascended the upper slopes and to his delight was able to collect about fifty varieties of alpine plants. Unlike others of the era, when Borgeau got a chance to name a peak he preferred to choose a name based on a natural feature rather than use the name of a person who more often than not would probably never even see the peak.

Raymond Patterson, who disapproved of many of the names chosen by A. O. Wheeler would probably have approved of Bourgeau's choices. However, in 1928 the mountain was renamed in honour of Sir James Lougheed.

Eugene Bourgeau (Saskatchewan Archives Board)

MT. LOUGHEED

Sir James, who practiced law in Calgary in partnership with the future Prime Minister R. B. Bennet, was appointed to the senate and later became a government minister. His grandson Peter was Premier of Alberta in the 1970's and early 1980's, and during his time in office succeeded, with other members of his family, in climbing the mountain with guides; a fairly difficult ascent.

Hon. James Lougheed in 1911
(Glenbow Archives)

The renaming of the mountain in 1928 was not the end of the name "Wind." The massive mountain which dominates the view from Dead Man Flat on the Trans-Canada Highway is the northwestern peak of a set of four, all of which appear on the Panorama and are approximately the same elevation. To the south is another summit of Lougheed and farther to the south still lies a quite spectacular tower which was named Wind Mountain in 1985.

So there still is a Wind Mountain but it is not the mountain Bourgeau named Wind in 1858. To further complicate matters, the steep-cliffed mountain to the right of Mount Lougheed is known as Wind Tower and the ridge immediately southwest of Dead Man Flat is called Wind Ridge.

Mount Lougheed is quite easily identifiable on the Panorama as the northernmost pair of peaks in the group which includes Mounts Sparrowhawk and Wind. The skyline becomes noticeably lower to the right of steep slopes below the northern summit.

Tom Wilson (Glenbow Archives)

The mountain we now know as Lougheed was still called Wind in 1889 when W. S. Drewry and A. St. Cyr claimed the first ascent. This was disputed in later years by none other than Tom Wilson, the most famous of the early packers and outfitters of Banff National Park, who claimed to have climbed the mountain two days earlier. Wilson, Drewry, and St. Cyr were all in the employ of J. J. McArthur, Dominion Land Surveyor, at the time.

View to the south from Dead Man Flat on the Trans-Canada Highway, 20.4 km west of the junction with Highway #40

"As God is my judge I never in all my explorations saw such a matchless scene", was how Tom Wilson recalled the day in 1882 when, accompanied by his Indian guide Gold Seeker, he first saw Lake Louise. But Wilson's explorations in the mountains did not end with the discovery of Lake Louise. He worked as a guide, outfitter, and businessman in Banff for many years, discovering Emerald Lake in Yoho National Park and leading the first party into the Mount Assiniboine area in 1893. Wilson was active in the mountains until 1920 when he moved to Vancouver. However, the old lure proved too strong and he returned to spend the years from 1927 to 1933 providing "local colour" for the CPR by entertaining guests at the Banff Springs Hotel with stories of the old days.

Dead Man Flat on the Trans-Canada Highway provides an ideal viewpoint for Mount Lougheed which dominates the view to the south and is often seen with clouds swirling around the summit as they were that day in 1858 when Bourgeau collected his wildflowers and named it Wind Mountain.

MOUNT LORETTE
2,484 m 74 km

Mount Lorette lies northwest of the point where the Kananaskis Valley becomes quite narrow, 10 km south of the University of Calgary's facilities at Barrier Lake. To the west of the mountain a power transmission line crosses Skogan Pass to Dead Man Flat on the Trans-Canada Highway.

Although Lorette is a very prominent peak, there is a second peak 1.8 km to the northwest which is 200 m higher. This is the peak which forms part of the Panorama seen from Nose Hill. It is not clear whether this higher point as well as the peak we see above the narrow part of the valley are both part of Mount Lorette, or if the higher summit is an unnamed mountain.

The tranquil view of the Kananaskis River with the steeply dipping limestones of Mount Lorette in the background is in marked contrast, to say the least, with what the Canadian soldier saw on Lorette Spur during World War I.

Canadian troops "going over the top" (National Archives of Canada)

View to the north from Highway #40, 2.6 km south of the Nakiska access road

On Easter Monday in 1917, four divisions of the Canadian Army attacked and held the most heavily defended German position on the Western Front. The French and British had both attempted to take Vimy Ridge and both had failed at tremendous cost, the French alone having lost 150,000 men. On this occasion, the Canadians went over the top at dawn and captured the ridge by noon, establishing new positions on the top of the Ridge as well as, some say, a new image of Canada to the world and in the eyes of the Canadian people themselves. Lorette Spur, a high point just to the north of Vimy Ridge and separated from it by the Souchez River was captured from the Germans by the French Army which suffered extremely high causalities in the battle. Pierre Berton, in his book "Vimy" relates a Canadian soldier's description of the carnage on Lorette Spur, "*It made his flesh crawl: he had never before seen so many grinning skulls. Here was a maze of old trenches and ditches littered with the garbage of war-broken rifles, frayed equipment, rusting bayonets, hundreds of bombs, tangles of barbed wire, puddles of filth, and everywhere rotting uniforms, some French blue, others German grey, tattered sacks now, holding their own consignments of bones.*"

The capture of Lorette Spur was a significant event in French military history. However, one questions why a prominent mountain in the Canadian Rockies was named in honour of this battle. One must travel south, almost to the US border in Waterton National Park in order to see Vimy Ridge and Vimy Mountain which were named for the battle in which the Canadian Army triumphed.

THE THREE SISTERS
2,970 m 88 km

Although not nearly as distinctive or picturesque as when viewed from Canmore, this well known group is easily recognizable from Calgary, all three peaks being visible through the valley made by the Bow River as it cuts through the front ranges.

Although James Hector did not name the mountains, the geologist of the Palliser Expedition clearly appreciated the view from the present day site of Canmore and wrote in his diary, *"Towards evening an excellent camping place was reached opposite a mountain with three peaks, which forms a very imposing group. In a nearby clearing we made camp and stayed for several days making a geological study of the rock formation."*

It was a brother of Major Rogers, the discoverer of Roger's Pass in the Selkirk Mountains, who named the mountains in 1883. He recalled, *"There had been quite a heavy snowstorm in the night, and when we got up in the morning and looked out of the tent I noticed each of the three peaks had a heavy veil of snow on the north side and I said to the boys,'Look at the Three Nuns'. They were called the Three Nuns for quite a while but later were called the 'Three Sisters', more Protestant like I suppose."*

The highest of the Three Sisters was first climbed in 1887 by the surveyor J. J. McArthur. The lowest is a much more difficult ascent and was not climbed until 1925 by a party led by Canmore's most illustrious mountain man Lawrence Grassi.

THE THREE SISTERS

View to the south from near Canmore on the Trans-Canada Highway

Grassi emigrated to Canada from Italy, coming to Canmore to work in the coal mines in 1916. By 1938 he had an impressive record, not only as a coal miner but also as a climbing guide, having made many lone ascents of difficult peaks. In a speech to the House of Commons supporting the naming of two lakes after Lawrence Grassi, Dr. J. S. Woodsworth said, *"Last summer I spent a month in a little mountain town in the Rockies. For me, the most interesting individual in the community was Lawrence Grassi, an Italian miner. In the course of a prolonged strike, instead of loafing about the village, he set off into the hills, axe on shoulder, to make trails to points of interest. It was a labour of love. He loved the mountains but enjoyed having others share their beauty. So day by day he pushed through the bush discovering the best ways of approach - blazing a trail, cutting out the underbrush, grubbing out stones and rocks, bridging little mountain streams....".*

Lawrence Grassi in front of his house in Canmore, 1950 (Whyte museum of the Canadian Rockies)

After he retired, Grassi's career was by no means over. He is probably best known for the trails he built in the Lake O'Hara area where he worked as a park warden in his later years. His beautiful rockwork will be used by generations of hikers to reach the high valleys of Lake Oesa and Lake McArthur.

Clearly, there is no better viewpoint for the Three Sisters than from Grassi's home town of Canmore.

GROTTO MOUNTAIN
2,706 m 82 km

When travelling from Calgary to Banff, one heads west-southwest when first entering the front range. Upon reaching Dead Man Flat and the south end of the Fairholm Range, the highway turns almost ninety degrees northwest towards Banff. The peak at the southernmost end of the Fairholm Range in the angle of the highway is Grotto Mountain, named by Eugene Bourgeau for the large, high-roofed cave he explored with James Hector. Hector and Bourgeau of the Palliser Expedition, had gone exploring above timberline on the mountain, following a creek to its source where a high waterfall plunged into a clear pool.

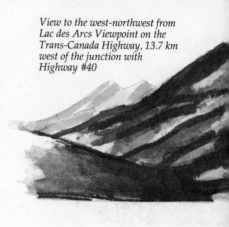

View to the west-northwest from Lac des Arcs Viewpoint on the Trans-Canada Highway, 13.7 km west of the junction with Highway #40

Grotto Mountain is not as tranquil a spot as it was that day in 1858 when Hector and Bougeau performed their morning ablutions at the pool below the waterfall. Much of the lower portion of the mountain is slowly being quarried away to be made into cement. A recent rockslide on the upper part of the mountain above the portion being removed may be related to the activity below.

Edwin Loder 1866
(Glenbow Archives)

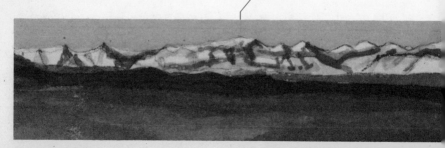

When the Canadian Pacific Railway arrived at the foot of the mountain in 1884, a Scot named McCanleish was already operating pot kilns to extract lime. After McCanleish mysteriously failed to return from a routine trip to Calgary, one of his employees named Edwin Loder obtained squatter's rights to the property and the operation carried on as Loder Lime Company until it was sold in 1952.

The Loder's large home became the social centre for the community of Exshaw (which lies just to the east of Grotto), the entire community being invited to Christmas Dinner each year. After the meal, the children were put to bed and the parlour cleared of furniture for dancing to the music provided by a player piano. Loder Peak to the northeast of Exshaw is a small mountain on the front range named in honour of this pioneer family of the Bow Valley.

Another quarry on the slopes of Grotto Mountain was started by a Mr. Butchart who left the area in 1908 to start the Butchart Quarry on Vancouver Island. When quarrying was completed at this site, it was transformed into the famous Butchart Gardens, one of the most popular attractions in the Victoria area.

ASSOCIATION PEAK

MOUNT JOHN LAURIE (YAMNUSKA)
2,240 m 72 km

Binoculars and a very clear morning are required to spot this popular rock climbing challenge from Nose Hill. Located on the north side of the Bow River, Mount John Laurie is the most easterly mountain in the valley and features a very steep, often vertical and overhanging south cliff 360 m in height and almost 2 km in width.

The rock is a very hard, 500 million year old limestone of Cambrian Period which does not erode easily and thus forms cliffs. Beneath this very old rock lies comparatively young layers of sandstone, mudstone, and siltstone of the Cretaceous Period (only 65 to 80 million years old) which erode much more easily and form the gentle slopes below the cliff.

The major thrust fault along which the older rock was pushed to its present position on top of the younger rock is called the McConnell Fault after R. G. McConnell who first mapped this major geologic feature.

Moose Mountain, Prairie Mountain, and Forget-Me-Not Ridge are the only features on the Panorama lying east of the McConnell Thrust Fault which marks the eastern edge of the front ranges over a considerable distance.

Generally sound rock combined with easy access from Calgary and a southerly exposure which makes it climbable when most other mountains are not in condition has made the mountain very popular with serious, technical climbers. Rock climbing history on Mount John Laurie began in the 1950's when guides Hans Gmoser and Leo Grillmair arrived from Europe and put up "Grillmair Chimney" route. There are now over three dozen recognized climbs with modern, less conventional names such as "Mum's Tears"."Freakout", "Gollem Grooves", "Feeding Frenzy", "Max Headroom", and "New Hope for the Dead".

Pioneer Hans Gmoser on "Red Shirt"
(Photo Hans Gmoser)

MT. JOHN LAURIE

Until 1961 the mountain was known as Yamnuska, which describes the features in the Stoney Indian Language. It was renamed at the request of the Stoneys in honour of the founder of the Indian Association of Alberta, John Laurie.

Laurie was a teacher who concerned himself with the lack of educational opportunities available to western Indians by offering to teach the families of his Indian and rancher friends in return for board and whatever salary they could pay. Over the years he assisted the Indians in many other ways, primarily in the area of legal matters, and in their relations with the Government.

The following inscription appears on a large rock on the Stoney Reserve beneath Mount John Laurie: *"A good friend to the Indians who taught them to preserve their culture and their treaty rights, and helped the nine tribes of our province into the Indian Association of Alberta. His efforts improved the condition of the Indian, and created friendship, equality, and understanding between our Alberta Indians and other citizens. Over the boundaries of colour and race swept the will of the Great Spirit."*

John Laurie (Glenbow Archives)

View to the northwest from Seebee Dam on Highway #1X

Mount John Laurie may be seen for a considerable distance as one travels towards the mountains along the Trans-Canada Highway.

ASSOCIATION PEAK & END MOUNTAIN
2,332 m 74 km & 2,420 m 73 km

To the north of Mount John Laurie lies a small, two-mountain range located 5 km to the east of the front range between the headwaters of Old Fort Creek and the South Ghost River.

Association Peak is the southernmost and lower of the two although it is just tall enough to form a small portion of the skyline on the Panorama. From the Bow Valley it is an attractive, symmetric peak which because of its prominent location east of the main range is quite noticeable from the Trans-Canada Highway.

Unfortunately, the Association for which the peak was named is not known.

Although almost 100 m higher than Association Peak, End Mountain does not appear on the skyline when viewed from Nose Hill. An unspectacular peak, it must have been of some significance to early travellers in the area because it was named as early as 1884, presumably because it forms the northern end of the small range.

View of Association Peak (left) and End Mountain (centre), looking northwest from the Trans-Canada Highway, 9.8 km west of the Morley Overpass

ASSOCIATION PEAK

SADDLE PEAK
(2,831 m 80 km)

View of Saddle Peak (centre left), looking west from Highway #940 5.8 km west of Benchlands

Saddle Peak, Orient Point and Mount Aylmer are the only three peaks seen from Nose Hill which lie within Banff National Park. Saddle Peak is the southernmost of the three and is situated on the park boundary between the valley containing Lake Minnewanka and the South Ghost River. When viewed from Nose Hill as well as from other locations north of the Bow Valley, it is most easily identified by noting its position behind and to the left of Orient Point.

There are at least two other mountains in southern Alberta named after their resemblance to a saddle. Perhaps the best known is the Saddle Peak which lies adjacent to The Saddleback above Lake Louise. The least known, but the one which best suits the name, is a small mountain just east of Mount Livingstone near the southern end of the Panorama.

ORIENT POINT
2,636 m 76 km

For a mountain to have been named Orient Point suggests that its location must have been significant to early travellers. It was certainly significant to Sir George Simpson, the first white man to travel through Devil's Gap on his way to becoming Banff's first visitor.

Orient Point rises to the south of this infrequently travelled route through the front ranges. As well as being the most easterly peak in Banff National Park, the mountain is significant in that it marks the eastern entrance to what is commonly known as the Lake Minnewanka Valley. Once one becomes familiar with the shape of Orient Point and its prominent position south of Devil's Gap, it becomes quite easy to identify and the reason for its name becomes apparent.

It is interesting to note that prior to the last major ice age, the Bow River did not flow eastward from Banff below the cliffs of Mount Rundle and past the present site of Canmore to the plains. Rather it followed the valley now occupied by Lake Minnewanka, passing through Devil's Gap to the north of Orient Point into the present day Ghost River Valley and then following the Bow Valley to Calgary.

View to the southwest from Highway #940, 4.7 km west of Ghost River Ranger Station

As governor of the Hudson's Bay Company, Sir George Simpson was probably the most powerful man in British North America at the time. He was combining business with adventure when he passed this way in August, 1841 with twenty-two men and forty-five horses, for although Simpson was interested in expanding the HBC's fur empire, he was also on a trip around the world.

The party was guided by a half breed chief of the mountain Cree named Peechee who is commemorated by the peak which lies to the south of Lake Minnewanka's mid point.

Sir George Simpson (Glenbow Archives)

Simpson wrote that, *"The Indians and Peechee were the only persons that had ever pursued this route; and we were the first whites that had attempted this pass in the mountains."* The pass is now known as Devil's Gap. Simpson referred to the mountains on either side as, *"very grand, of every varied form... their craggy summits resembling battlements among which dizzy heights the goat and sheep delight to bound."*

ORIENT POINT

MOUNT AYLMER
3,162 m 96 km

With an elevation of 3,162 m, Mount Aylmer is the tallest peak north of the Bow River seen from the Nose Hill vantage point. Lying 5 km north of the west end of Lake Minnewanka near the headwaters of the Ghost River, it is at 96 km the most distant mountain readily identifiable from Calgary with the exception of the peaks south of the Highwood River. The upper portion appears just to the right of Orient Point on the Panorama but is 20 km farther west and 526 m higher. Mount Aylmer often has snow on its summit when lower elevation mountains in front are bare and is most easily identified under these conditions.

A most impressive viewpoint for Mount Aylmer is from the townsite of Banff. The peak lies to the northeast and rises dome-like behind the mountains of the Palliser Range with a profile quite similar to that seen from Nose Hill although much larger since the mountain is only 18 km distant.

It is most unusual that a mountain should be named by the person who made the first ascent. J. J. McArthur named the peak after his native town of Aylmer, Quebec which is located at Lac Deschenes on the Ottawa River some 10 km southeast of Hull.

McArthur was a Dominion Land Surveyor who worked from 1886 to 1893 completing a topographic survey of the Rocky Mountains along the Canadian Pacific Railway's main line. Tom Wilson was hired by McArthur as a packer and in addition to caring for the surveyor and his horses and supplies, Wilson often assisted in carrying the bulky twenty pound camera and plates as well as the fifteen pound transit to the summit of mountains chosen as photographic stations.

MT. AYLMER

View to the northeast looking along Banff Avenue from the corner of Elk Street, Banff

McArthur mapped 2,000 square miles at a scale of 1:20,000 and contour interval of 100 feet. In the course of this detailed work, he made some of the earliest first ascents in the Rockies including such well known peaks as Rundle, Bourgeau, Stephen, and the highest of the Three Sisters.

A. O. Wheeler wrote of McArthur: *"He is a quiet, unassuming man, who has probably climbed more mountains in these regions than any other person.... In all kinds of weather, through snow, over ice, and in pouring rain, many a difficult ascent has been accomplished, many privations encountered and much hardship endured; the only record being a few terse paragraphs in the Departmental Bluebook..."*.

For many years J. J. McArthur was the authority on the Rockies west of Calgary.

James J. McArthur (National Archives of Canada)

DEVIL'S HEAD
2,796 m 86 km

If a Calgarian can recognize one mountain from the Panorama, it is probably Devil's Head. Its distinctive shape formed by 250-metre cliffs on the north, east, and south sides of a fairly flat-topped summit remains consistent from all viewpoints north of the Bow River. These cliffs are near vertical, so that following a snowfall, Devil's Head remains black while surrounding mountains are white. It is under these conditions that the mountain is most impressive.

Once Devil's Head is identified, it is interesting to try to pick out Blackrock Mountain which lies 8 km to the east but is 322 m lower in elevation and does not form part of the skyline on the Panorama.

Devil's Head from Blackrock Mountain (Photo Gillean Daffern)

The name Devil's Head is a translation of the Stoney Indian name based on the mountain's shape.

View to the west from Highway #940, 12.9 km west of the junction with Highway #1A

DEVIL'S HEAD

W. S. Drewry, an assistant to J. J. McArthur, attempted to climb the mountain in 1891 while in the area surveying, but was turned back by the precipices below the summit. The peak's challenging cliffs must have been noticed by all the early mountaineers as they journeyed by train to make first ascents in the more spectacular main ranges of the Rockies during the early part of this century. However, Devil's Head's somewhat isolated location and distance from the railway combined to delay the first ascent until 1925 when J. W. A. Hickson and L. S. Crosby climbed the mountain from the west, guided by the man who made more first ascents in the Rockies and Selkirks than any other climber.

Edward Feuz Jr. was the son of one of the first guides brought to Canada from Switzerland by the CPR During the 1890's, the president of the railway, William Van Horne, was attempting to promote a program of attracting tourists to the Rockies and the CPR's hotels and one of his ideas was to supply guides for mountaineering parties.

When Edward Jr. arrived in Canada in 1903, he apprenticed under his father and began work at Glacier House near Roger's Pass for the CPR for whom he continued to work until his retirement in 1949. He is credited with being the first person to stand upon the summit of 78 peaks and with leading 102 new climbing routes, all without a fatal accident. When based at Lake Louise he was involved in the building of the "Swiss style" alpine hut on Abbot's Pass at an elevation approaching 3000 m, some 200 m higher than the elevation of Devil's Head. In keeping with the era, Edward always felt that a guide was integral to climbing no matter how competent the climbers. Even Sir Edward Whymper, famous for his first ascent of the Matterhorn, climbed with a guide when he visited the Canadian Rockies.

The first ascent of Devil's Head was one of the few climbs Edward Feuz Jr. made in the front ranges and may have been the only time this legendary alpine guide would have gazed to the east to try and spot the City of Calgary.

Edward Feuz Jr. c. 1915 (Whyte Museum of the Canadian Rockies)

Lying 10 km north of the east end of Lake Minnewanka, Devil's Head is the only named peak in a group of mountains situated between the Waiparous River to the north and the Ghost River to the south.

BLACKROCK MOUNTAIN
2,472 m 78 km

The mountain is not high and is often difficult to identify from Nose Hill as it does not form part of the skyline panorama. However, when storm clouds lie between Blackrock and the front ranges farther west, it is often the only mountain visible from Calgary. It is under these conditions, with clouds behind it, that the mountain appears black and this is probably the reason for its name. A similar phenomenon occurs when the main front range receives a snowfall but Blackrock does not.

The most unique feature of Blackrock Mountain is its somewhat isolated location. Almost all of the mountains we see from Calgary are more or less neatly lined up in ranges which are oriented along a NNE-SSW trend. Blackrock, however, rises some 5 km to the east of the front range with no other peaks to the north or south.

The type of rock of which the mountain is made is no different from the nearby mountains, so it is doubtful that the colour was involved in the naming. However, the age of the rock which forms Blackrock Mountain is unique amongst all mountains visible from Calgary because it is the oldest. It is made up of the Cathedral Formation of Middle Cambrian Period, the sediments being laid down in shallow seas about 550 million years ago.

View to the north from the Trans-Canada Highway, 9.8 km west of the Morley overpass

The mountain's position east of the front ranges may best be seen by looking north from the Trans-Canada Highway at Morley Flats.

BLACKROCK MTN

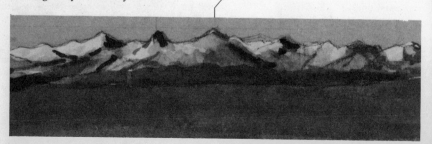

*Devil's Head and the Blackrock Lookout
(Photo Jack Carter; courtesy Milt Magee)*

Blackrock Mountain's special location was noticed by the Alberta Forest Service when choosing locations for its initial series of fire lookouts during the late 1920's. A relatively high mountain set somewhat east of the main front range provides an ideal viewpoint of forested foothills to the north, east, and south. Built on the very summit during 1929 and tethered to the site by cables, the wooden lookout building was manned during summer months by lookouts who communicated with the forest rangers below by telephone cable, some of which remains on the mountain today. For the 30 years it was in operation, the lookout was supplied by packhorses. An impressive amount of rockwork had to be done in order to build a horse trail up steep scree slopes providing a route through the cliffs near the summit.

Today, the building still stands on what is probably the most exposed building site in Canada and the horse trail remains as well, both testifying to some fine workmanship by men who must have been very aware of the difficulties involved in building and servicing a residence on top of a mountain.

The lookout was closed in 1952, replaced by two others: Mockingbird and Burnt Timber at considerably lower elevations. The lower locations were much more easily serviced and less likely to be in the clouds and thus ineffective for the spotting of smoke.

Anyone who has stood at the front door of the wooden building clinging to the summit cannot fail to be impressed by the history associated with the old lookout on Blackrock.

INDEX OF PEAKS

Allan, Mount 72, 73

Association Peak 86

Aylmer, Mount 90, 91

Banded Peak 44

Blackrock Mountain 94, 95

Blane, Mount 51, 52

Bluerock Mountain 31

Bogart, Mount 67, 68

Brock, Mount 53

Burke, Mount 17

Burns, Mount 34, 35, 36

Coffin Mountain 12

Cornwall, Mount 48, 49

Cougar Mountain 39

Devil's Head 92, 93

Elpoca Mountain 45, 46

End Mountain 86

Evan-Thomas, Mount 57

Fisher Peak 58

Foch, Mount 42, 43

Forget-Me-Not Mountain 40, 41

Gibraltar Mountain 26, 27

Glasgow, Mount 48, 49, 50

Gass, Mount 19

Grotto Mountain 82, 83

Hailstone Butte 14

Head, Mount 22, 23

Holy Cross Mountain 20, 21

Hood, Mount 54, 55

Howard, Mount 61

John Laurie, Mount 84, 85

Junction Mountain 25

Kidd, Mount 65, 66

Livingstone, Mount 13

Lorette, Mount 78, 79

Lougheed, Mount 74, 75, 76, 77

Lyall, Mount 18

McDougall, Mount 64

Mist Mountain 28, 29, 30

Moose Mountain 62, 63

Nihahi Ridge 60

Orient Point 88, 89

Plateau Mountain 15, 16

Prairie Mountain 59

Pyriform, Mount 24

Rae, Mount 37, 38

Remus, Mount 56

Romulus, Mount 56

Saddle Peak 87

Sparrowhawk, Mount 69, 70

Storm Mountain 32, 33

The Three Sisters 80, 81

Tombstone Mountain 47

Wind Mountain 71

Yamnuska 84, 85

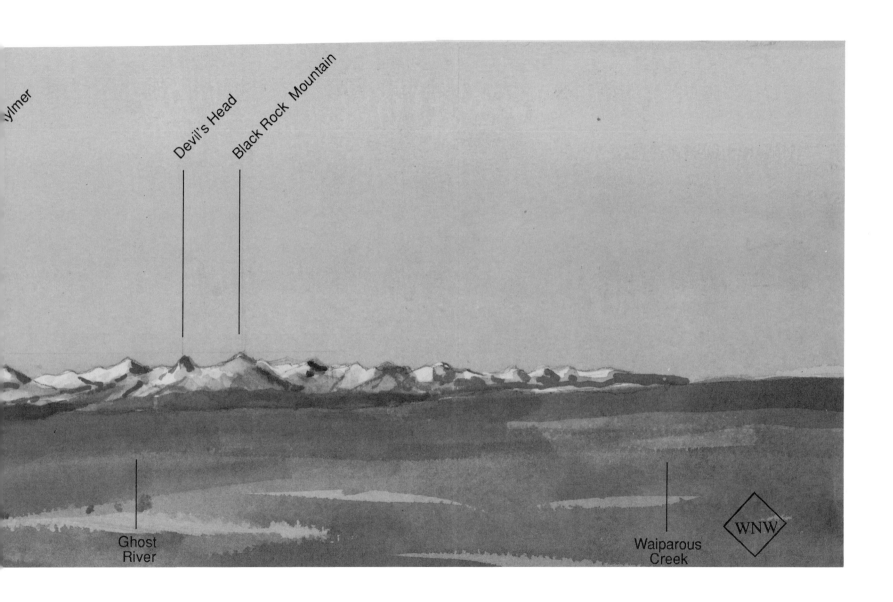

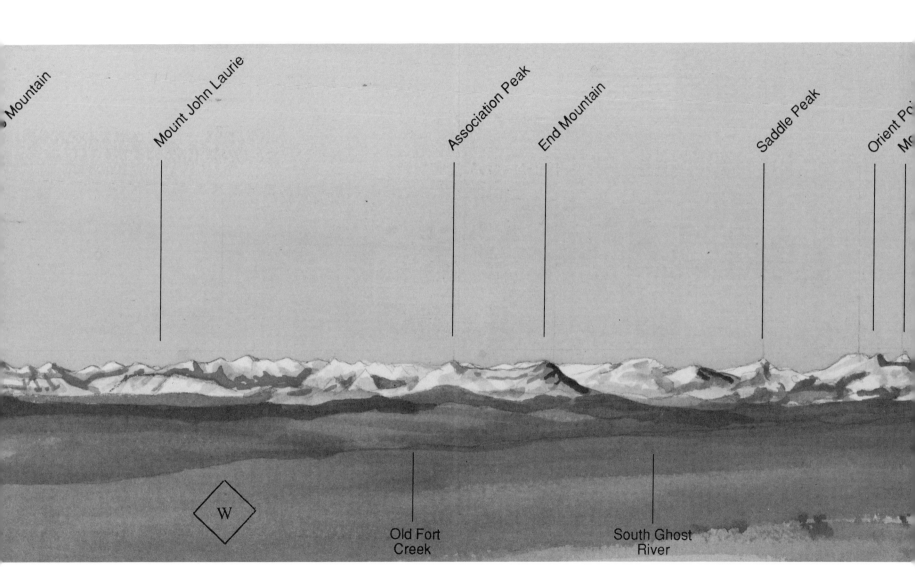

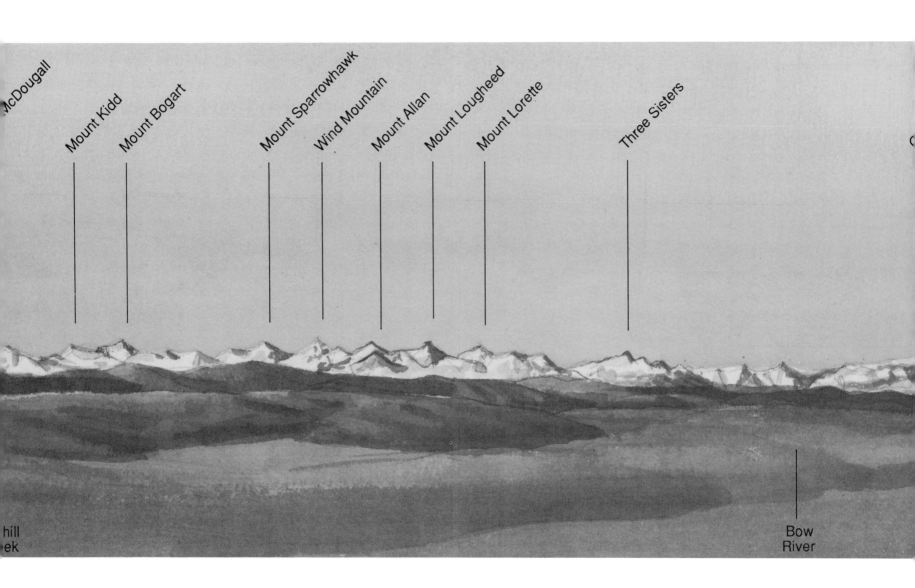

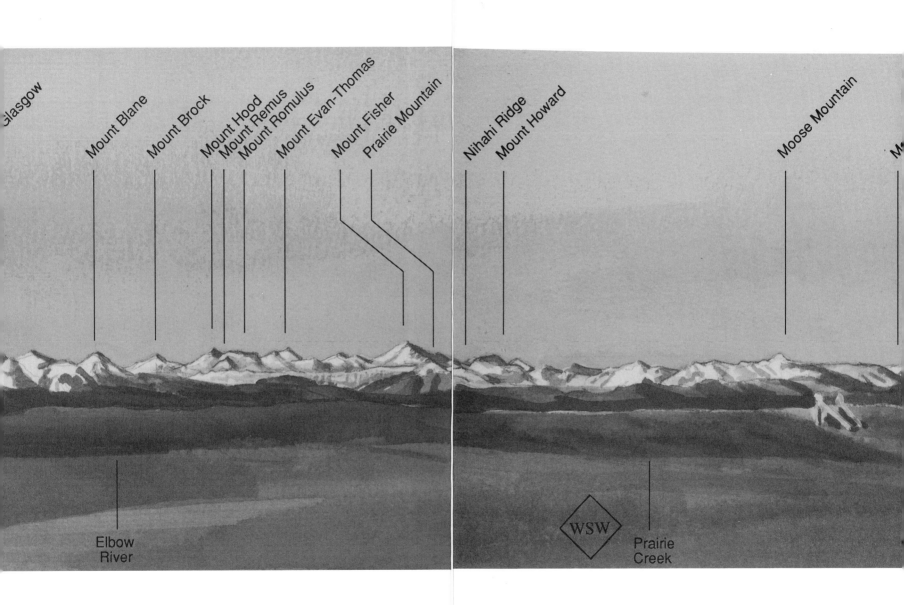

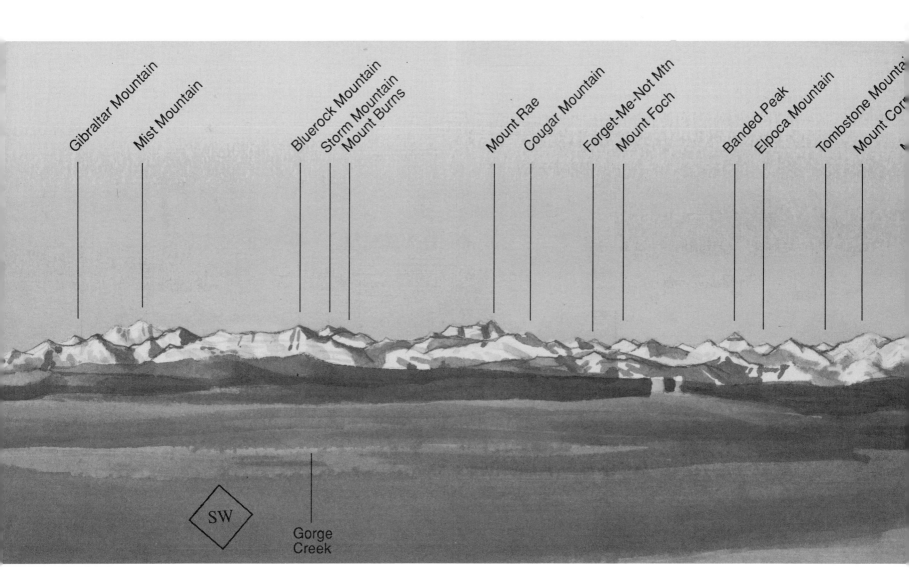

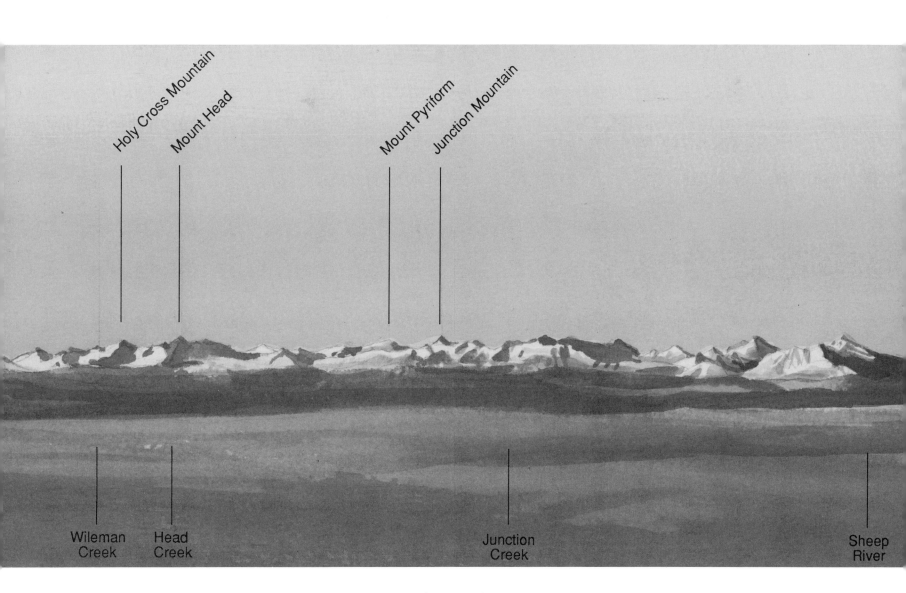

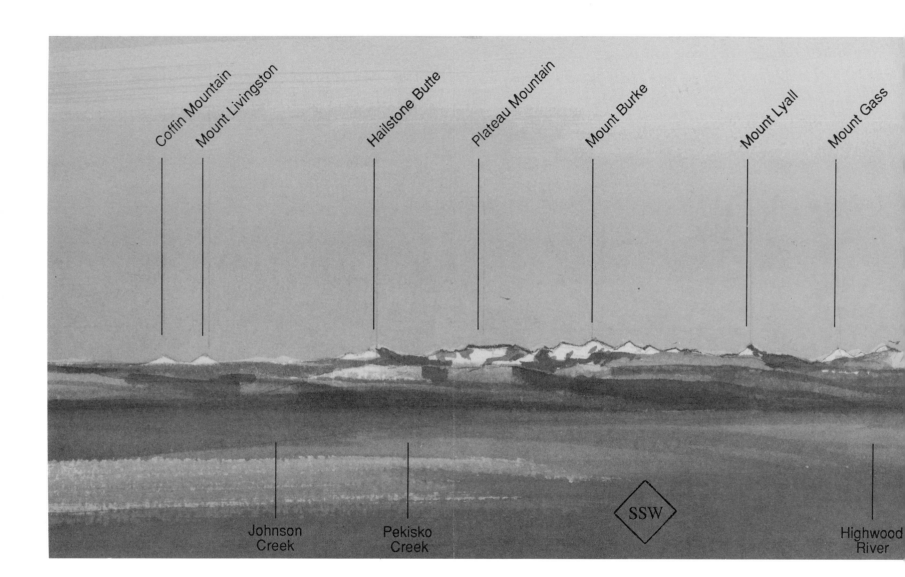